HOW TO SURVIVE WOMEN

A MAN'S GUIDE

7 SIMPLE STEPS THAT WORK

K.M. KNOWLES

OSBORNE STEWART

Published by Osborne Stewart

LIBRARY OF CONGRESS CATALOGING-IN-PUBLICATION DATA
How to Survive Women: A Man's Guide. Seven Simple Steps That Work by K.M. Knowles. -- 1st ed.
ISBN 978-0-9919720-0-5

Cover design and interior graphics by Murray Grelis, Badaboom Graphic Design
Editing by Jennifer Ciotta, Pencey X Pages

Printed in the United States of America
First Printing, 2013
ISBN 978-0-9919720-0-5

Dedicated to my toughest critics and biggest fans,
Eamon and Madeleine Knowles

CONTENTS

INTRODUCTION

INTRODUCTION

A lot has been written about women. Some of it is helpful—and is supported by research, studies, and analysis—but most of it isn't. In my experience, because most men are not particularly interested in research, studies, and analysis, the "helpful" material stays on a shelf, and men continue to be confounded by women.

This book distills armloads of "helpful" material into seven simple steps to help you to be less confounded by women. (It's tempting to make the wild promise that this book will also help you understand women, but that's beyond the reach of most of us.)

The seven steps provide a framework so that theory nerds get their fix. More importantly, the seven steps provide you with a roadmap to understanding the seemingly elusive forces that are at work when you're relating to women and which bite you in the ass without warning (both the elusive forces and the women).

You'll find tools that you can use immediately to improve your relationships with women. You can turn to any chapter to find a quick technique to survive—and thrive with—women, from handling the "we need to talk" command to the seven-minute rule.

The focus of this book is the most important woman in your life: your *Mate*. This delightful multipurpose word refers to a friend or buddy in Australia ("G'day, mate") and in the U.K. In nature it refers to a sexual partner. For men, the definition of a happy, stable long-term relationship usually involves both of these: a happy Mate and some action in the sack.

Lack of sex is often a litmus test for men to measure how unhappy their relationship is.

If the relationship is bad, sex is 80 per cent of the problem.

If the relationship is good, sex gets 20 per cent of the credit.

This book shows you what gets the other 80 per cent of the credit in a good relationship. Turning up the volume on that 80 per cent is the secret to having a great relationship because it builds emotional connection, which is a woman's litmus test of a happy relationship.

The goal for men is to turn up the volume with the least amount of effort because—let's be honest—there are only so many hours in the day. This book explains how to raise the volume, from ensuring the perfect gift for her with your cell phone to mastering three words to help you sidestep a week in the doghouse. (Hint: those words are *not* "I love you.")

If you can develop a great relationship with your Mate, you are on your way to having great relationships with other women in your orbit: your daughter, your boss, your clients, your friends' Mates, and the vice president of human resources who is reviewing your pay increase, or more importantly, the latest round of job cuts.

The stakes are high. Not only are you surrounded by females, you are outnumbered. On a sober note, over 50 per cent of American marriages end in divorce within seven years, rising to 67 per cent—a shocking two out of three—by the 40th wedding anniversary.[1] Twice as many men are choosing *not* to marry rather than make a mistake, compared to 25 years ago. Three-fourths of these men are not so much terrified of marriage but of the wrong woman and what a bad divorce could do to them.

This book helps you get a handle on whether you (or your sons) are dating the wrong woman. It also explains women whom I call *Dragons*. You may know them as queen bees, prima donnas, or just plain ol' bitches. Regardless of what you call them, they should be avoided at your peril. This book shows you how. This is an equal opportunity book: the male equivalent of a Dragon is a *Douche*, and he gets a turn under the microscope too.

While the stakes are high, the benefits of a long-term and stable relationship are also high: people who get married—and stay married—live four years longer than people who don't. They get sick less often, are financially better off, and are happier.

If you want some of that, let's get on with it.

STEP 1

Choose Well

BE GREAT OR GO SOLO

10,000 hours. That's how long it takes to achieve greatness.

This theory, according to Malcolm Gladwell in his book *Outliers*, factors in some modicum of talent combined with *a lot* of practice to be great. Think Tiger Woods on the golf course and how many decades of work it took for him to achieve greatness in the sport. That's what you're striving for in a relationship with a woman.

Now let's assume that great relationships are the result of some modicum of talent (thereby disqualifying Douches and Dragons at the starting line) *and* a lot of practice. Applying Gladwell's 10,000-hours rule to the average couple who spends a whopping four minutes a day together[2], uninterrupted, a great relationship could be achieved after *411 years* of dedicated practice. Thank goodness for "until death do us part."

Let's assume you didn't set out to have an "average" marriage, or even a merely "good" one. (Seriously, why bother? Stay single and be awesome rather than married and mediocre.) Let's assume you are *above* average, and that you set out to have a great relationship by finding yourself a great woman and being her great partner.

Now let's quantify how above average you are. How about *seven and a half times* above average?

If this were true, you would spend 30 minutes a day together, uninterrupted (dinner at the dining table? commuting together?). What if you stepped it up to three hours a day on weekends (a dinner date? cleaning out the garage together? nine holes of golf as a twosome?) This is not to be confused with merely showing up and sharing the same airspace, much like preschoolers who play side by side silently. Rather, you are actively engaged with your Mate in conversation and sharing. With this advanced level of "practice," you and your Mate might hope to achieve greatness in a mere *35 years*.

You may know a rare couple like this, such as the man and woman who walk their ancient dog together. He holds the door open for her at the bank, or they drive to the store, happy and waving to all the neighbors, in their pristine and sensible car of a certain vintage. It's delightfully reassuring to be around people like this. Rather like holding a newborn or watching a dog launch itself joyfully into play, we are reassured that the world is a good place to be.

But great relationships don't simply *happen*. They take talent—two willing, good hearts—and practice. It's a long road with no shortcuts, but the rewards are worth the effort. In addition to being healthier, wealthier, and living longer, married men have more—and better—sex.[3]

LIKE MOTHER, LIKE DAUGHTER

When you get serious about someone, do yourself—and everyone you know, present and future—a massive favor. Choose the right woman.

Simple. But not easy.

How do you know if she's The One?

Before we get into that, take a look at what's at stake:

- Your assets
- Your future earnings
- Your relationships with your family
- Your relationships with your friends
- Where you'll live
- Even how long you'll live
- Your happiness, and that includes how much sex she will let you have *for the rest of your life.*

In short, you are betting your life on this woman, your Mate for life. You are also betting your kids' lives on her. So how do you know if she's the right one? Your for-the-rest-of-your-life Mate? Your *Diamond*? These sought-after gems have unparalleled durability, luster and value, and maybe a few flaws too. But the potential of Diamonds—women and men—to dazzle and endure is unmatched.

Start with her mother. In 10 years' time, this is the woman your Mate will probably become.

If you don't believe me, take a field trip to the closest shopping mall. Watch the parade of mothers and daughters shopping together. Be subtle, guys! You're *observing*, not stalking.

Dollars to donuts Mom and Daughter share similar body types. Not only do women often look like their mother, they frequently *act* like her.

Take her mom out for coffee and get a handle on this. There are women whose entire personality is constructed on the shortcomings of others: the unappreciative husband, the extra 15 pounds, the overbearing boss, the deranged dog next door, and the future son-in-law who fails to measure up.

Take a look at how she treats people who are serving her, especially waiters and waitresses. If she treats them with confidence and courtesy, looks at them with a smile when she places her order or gets a refill for her coffee, and doesn't make a sugarcoated snide comment about them when their backs are turned, you should be able to see these traits in her daughter.

Why is it important how Mom treats servers? Because if she doesn't notice their existence, in 10 years' time her daughter probably won't notice your existence either. Worse, if Mom treats them in an off-hand or dismissive manner, you could be on the receiving end of a supercilious and belittling attitude from your Mate in the future.

Observe Mom at family gatherings, especially the ones she hosts at her home. Is she is a stressed-out control freak who goes crazy when the weird uncle drinks too much and the dessert gets dropped? Or is she warmly greeting family and friends, delegating tasks to share the kitchen fun, and relaxing and laughing with her guests?

Next, take a close look at how Mom treats Dad, because that is probably how you will be treated by your Mate. Take Dad out for a drink and get a handle on his life with Mom. This guy is living with the woman who is the blueprint for your Mate. He bet *his* life on Mom. How is that working out for him? Is he content or henpecked? Are they great friends who respect each other, or does he talk wistfully about a pretty girl he used to know?

Now take all that information and ask yourself: Are you willing to bet your life on their daughter?

Don't despair if you don't like what you see. It's not a foregone conclusion that all daughters will morph into their moms. Darwin's theory of evolution comes into play; some daughters actively evolve and shed Mom's less-than-desirable traits, vowing to be exactly opposite to their mother. Other women with difficult or absent mothers may have chosen another female role model to emulate. Ask your Mate who most influenced her as she was growing up, and why. But you need to be realistic, because unless Daughter has decided otherwise, she is on a path to become her mother: the dreaded Mini-Mom.

The clue you are looking for—whether your life will be a haven of happiness with your Mate or hell on earth with Mini-Mom—lies with her mom's sense of self. Experts have identified that this is a critical element for the two of them to be able to separate from each other successfully and healthily.[4]

Without going Jung-Freudian on you, if Mom is confident in herself and her abilities, is comfortable with her life and surroundings, and possesses a centeredness that neither passes judgement on others nor is closed to opinions of others whom she knows well and trusts, then Mom's sense of self is doing pretty well.[5]

Chances are that a mom who is as together as this has raised a daughter who has her act together too.

TRUE OR FALSE:
SHE HATES YOUR DOG

So, you absolutely adore your new girlfriend, and everything is going swimmingly. Except for one tiny thing. She can't stand your dog.

She is not a dog hater; in fact, she says she loves dogs. Except your dog.

If only your dog wouldn't stink up the living room when you're watching a movie, pee on her handbag, or sleep on the bed. Or, for God's sake, watch balefully when you're having sex.

Maybe it's not your dog. It's your T-shirt collection that she doesn't care for. Or that you chew with your mouth open. Or that you leave your dirty underwear on the floor like a five-year-old.

No matter how much she loves you, *whatever irritates her now will be your kryptonite.*

You will be astonished by the unfairness of it all. Your inner voice will protest, "But honey, you knew I had questionable table manners/a stinky dog, a rockin' T-shirt collection/the house-keeping habits of a five-year-old when we met, and you were OK with it then. Now you just go on and on about it. You're being unreasonable."

Maybe she is. But perhaps you're being just the teensiest bit unreasonable too.

Take her and Stinky to the local dog park and watch. If your Mate genuinely loves dogs, she will interact happily and goofily with other dogs, and maybe Stinky *is* the problem. However, if your Mate shrieks and shies away from the joyful doggies, maybe *she* is the problem.

Re-examine the T-shirt collection. Is it age appropriate for a grown man to wear a shrunken, faded team shirt from his university glory days with the number 69 on it when he proudly struts around town with his hot new girlfriend? Save that bad boy for washing her car.

As for chewing with your mouth open, you know the right thing to do, so just grow up and do it. Problem solved.

Turn the underwear on the floor into a major win. Ask if she will come shopping with you to help choose a laundry hamper, because in the bedroom, you want her attention to be on *you*, not on the messy room.

Dragon alert: you're not giving her free rein to redecorate your man cave. Rather, you're smart enough to know that she will appreciate you not acting like a five-year-old. So toss your dirty clothes in the snazzy new hamper, and while you're at it, put some fresh sheets on the bed and look forward to some grown-up sex.

These are straightforward issues that two reasonable adults should be able to sort out, both now and in the future.

But you may find yourself playing whack-a-mole: every time you reasonably sort something out with your princess, something else pops up to take its place. It goes on and on and on. It's exhausting. Where did the fun girl go?

Either you turned into a Douche, or she turned into a Dragon. Or both. Your dog deserves better.

PRETTY PEOPLE

Some of us were good looking and popular in school. Most of us were not.

The Pretty People were so freaking lucky, right? They didn't have to put effort into making friends or being brainy, sporty, funny, or sweet. It was enough for the Pretty People to show up; by their mere presence, the Other Kids' sorry lives would be filled with sunshine. Pretty People could even get away with vapid personalities or behaving badly, because the Others wanted to be in the Pretty People's orbit more than anything.

The Others, the plain, awkward, and downright ugly ones, knew about being mocked, stupid, clumsy, or invisible. It sucked to be them. They had to work at being something—*anything*—to be noticed. So they worked at being brainy, sporty, funny, or sweet.

As one bookish and introverted surfer from Florida—with no surfer girlfriend in sight—lamented, "I didn't think I was cute enough to score without some backup," so he decided to become funny.

Fast forward 20 years. The Pretty People are not so pretty anymore. Middle age, gravity, and hair loss don't discriminate; they go after most everyone. That nerdy surfer funny guy from Florida? He is five-time Emmy award-winning actor and comedian, Kelsey

Grammar.[6] He has no trouble attracting Pretty Girls; he's been married to four of them.

The Others are also afflicted by middle age, etc., but let's be honest, there wasn't much at stake for them to lose. They were used to being plain and awkward, so gravity and baldness are no big deal. One more insult or injury to be shrugged off.

As the "looks" playing field levels off, the importance of other qualities emerges. Something interesting is happening with the Other Kids. Some of them are really good at being brainy, sporty, funny, or sweet. They emerge as front-runners in their careers with solid financials, rich personalities, and a great circle of friends and peers. They are *successful*. They are Diamonds.

We like and admire them, want to be their friends, and to hire them (or be hired by them). And if we choose well, we will find a loving and loyal Mate in their midst.

Something interesting is also happening with the Pretty People. No longer hot, they have to figure out how to be something—*anything*—to stay relevant. Some of them master this, but many don't.

So what becomes of the Pretty People who don't evolve, who cling to their gift of physical beauty as it fades under the inevitability of gravity, hair loss, and middle age? They suffer the same fate as the Other Kids who can't shrug off the insults and injuries of their youth and who use their downtrodden-ness as an excuse. The boys become Douches, and the women become Dragons.

It sucks to be them. Or, even worse, in a relationship with one. So if your potential Mate is a

Pretty Person, make sure that she has demonstrated some aptitude for evolution, because otherwise she will become angry and resentful as her looks fade. And guess whose fault it will be?

How to SPOT A DRAGON

HOW TO SPOT A DRAGON

When boy meets girl, boy thinks with an organ other than his brain. This is a fact of nature and yet is a leading cause of misery for men who are not Douches.

Poor selection is not a big deal when you're dating, as long as you're having more fun than not. But it's a disaster when you are ready for someone longer term. The world is littered with successful—but breathtakingly stupid—men who've hitched their wagon to a Dragon.

Here is how *not* to become one of them. This is your guide to Dragon spotting.

Is she comfortable in her skin?

A woman who likes herself possesses an inner confidence that is timelessly sexy. This isn't about shyness, because that is her with other people. This is about her with *herself*. Dragons have an inferiority complex that will exhaust you. Some clues:

- Is she a card-carrying member of the Pretty People? Go back one chapter and miss a turn.
- Does she seek approval for every outfit? A Dragon will expect flattery and compliments every time she heads out the door.

   (Even a sane woman may ask you if her ass looks fat in those pants, but she is letting you know that she expects a compliment once in a while, not every waking moment. If your otherwise sane Mate is asking this question, it's because she's overdue for some appreciation from you!)

- Does she spend more time in the bathroom than any other woman you have ever known? Taking the time to look attractive is a good thing, but if it takes longer for her to get ready than the time you actually spend together, there's a strong possibility a Dragon lurks under her glossy exterior.
- Does she refuse to let you look at her naked, with the lights on? Be realistic and appreciative. She's not 19 anymore. Neither are you, hot stuff. Turn off the lights, break out those candles your aunt gave you for a house-warming gift, and take a long, appreciative look at your gorgeous Mate. A Dragon will have already left the room.
- Is her Facebook profile dominated by photos of herself? Are her tweets the 140-character equivalent of LOOK AT ME!? What part of Dragon-in-the-making are you not seeing?
- Does she wear makeup to the beach? Does she have fake nails? Does she fire her hairstylist frequently? Any one of these is a warning light for a high-maintenance princess, but together, they are an ominous sign. And if your princess gets her hair feng shui'd, *r-u-n*.

Is she comfortable with her smarts?

Regardless of IQ scores, a woman who's comfortable with her smarts is able to hold her own in a conversation about almost anything. In contrast, a Dragon will go one of two ways: she either wants to talk about things of interest to *herself* or listens vapidly to your monologue, probably while texting her posse the breaking news about who's wearing what.

What if you manage to get a good chat underway and think things are going well? Ask yourself, "Does she want to get to know me, or is she interviewing me?" Beware of being screen tested for the role of provider and sperm donor.

Does she have a good heart?

An evolved Dragon may have eluded detection so far, especially if you are smitten by her looks and conversation, but the heart of a Dragon is hard to miss. Some clues:

- A Dragon treats check-out clerks and servers as if they're invisible. Or worse, like something to wipe off her elegant shoe.

- Take a look at her friends. A Dragon's female friends are less attractive and less accomplished than her. She doesn't so much hang out with them as holds court with her adoring fans, always the center of attention. A fun woman can be the life of the party, but a Dragon needs to be spotlit on the stage.

- Has she ever been single for any length of time? A Dragon is either a chronic dater—boyfriends are stepping stones, one after another without any space in between—or she is a chronic singleton, because she is so demanding that no man measures up to her high standards. Chronic daters don't know themselves, because they can only define their egos by their relationships with others.

- Look carefully for clues when she talks about her exes. How did they meet? What attracted her to him? What was great about him? What wasn't? Why did they break up? Is it always his fault? How long did they last? If you're hearing the same story over and over, odds are she's a Dragon.

When you think you're falling in love, it's time to take off your rose-colored glasses and step up to the plate: What do her friends and family have to say about her when she's not in the room? A Dragon will go crazy about this one, which begs the question: What is she hiding?

A word of warning: you are not spying! You *want* to know about her, scales and all, from people who love her. Because you think you love her too. Be honorable with whatever you hear, because if you act like a Douche, I will find out and pillory you in my next book, *How to Survive Men: A Woman's Guide—One of Us Is Wrong, and It Isn't Me.*

What does she care about?

A Diamond cares about her family and friends and is there for them when the shit hits the fan. Meanwhile, a Dragon loves to switch on the fan. Crises and dramas are her caffeine.

All women know the kind of attributes they are looking for in a man. A Diamond's list goes deep into his spirit; a Dragon's list goes deep into his wallet.

How's the sex?

If you've read sex-advice columnist Dan Savage, you will be familiar with the abbreviation *GGG*. It stands for "good, giving, and game," which is what we should strive to be for our sex partners and vice versa. Great sex partners are *good* in bed, *give* equal time and equal pleasure, and are *game* for anything—within reason. Dragons may be freaking awesome in bed initially, but it is all about them. Sex will be on their terms and for their pleasure, and you will pay the price.

Reality check

Note the order of this chapter so far: body, mind, heart, spirit. These come first. *Then* sex. That's not to say that sex isn't important. On the contrary. Sex is like oxygen: when you have it, you appreciate it, but when there isn't enough of it, you can't think of anything else. However, it is these first four elements—body, mind, heart, and spirit—which will sustain you and your Mate for the 99 per cent of time when you are *not* having sex.

What else?

You've done the groundwork and you think she passes your examination. Go ahead and make some notes. Yes, write down the things you like about her body, mind, heart, and spirit. Then sex. And finally the things her family and friends say about her. It can be a Pulitzer prize-winning essay or a few words typed into your phone, filed under M for Mate. (Your phone is password protected, right?) Collect your thoughts, write them down, and we'll revisit them soon.

ARE YOU READY?

You have put your Mate under a magnifying glass and searched for signs of an inner Dragon lying in wait to slay you. Her family and friends have dished on her, and you have established that her mother isn't a nightmare. You and your snazzy new laundry hamper are reasonably confident that she doesn't hate your dog. You are harmonious in the GGG department. In short, you are ready and willing to bet your life—body, mind, heart, and spirit—on her.

Not so fast.

There is one question that you still need to ask. Not of her, but of yourself.

Are *you* ready?

For love to stand a chance of success, there are two elements that need to be perfectly aligned. One is luck. Congratulations, you have hit the jackpot and fate has brought you and your Mate together.

But the other element is timing. It is one thing to have met the woman of your dreams. It is another thing to meet her when the timing is right to commit to a serious relationship with her.

You may be an awesome guy with everything going for him, but if your day or week runs along these lines, you'd best back up the truck.

1. Wake
2. Walk Stinky
3. Eat

4. Work
5. Gym
6. Family/Friends
7. Eat/Drink
8. Catch up on emails/watch TV/work some more
9. Think about sex/call girlfriend/have sex at her place because:

   (a) you have dirty underwear all over your floor (hamper is still wrapped in plastic somewhere, probably in your car);

   (b) you can leave when you're done;

   (c) you need a good night's sleep for the big golf weekend you and the boys have planned; or

   (d) all of the above.

None of this makes you a Douche. You are a regular guy, maybe even an awesome guy...*except* if you delude yourself into thinking that you're ready and willing to commit to a long-term relationship when your life follows this pattern.

Where, precisely, did you think a great relationship would fit in? Between waking and walking Stinky? On the couch while you flip between Facebook and crap TV? Or as arm candy at your Christmas office party, because you would like to walk the red carpet with a beautiful woman who is not your sister?

Get real. You don't have the wherewithal to commit four minutes a day to an *average* relationship, let alone the 30-plus minutes for a *great* one. Do yourself a favor, and stay in the casual dating pool. Yes, it can be exhausting out there in the single world, but it is neither as exhausting nor as expensive as committing yourself to a relationship that you don't have room for.

SOME BIG QUESTIONS

It's time to ask yourself some big questions. About you. About her. About your life together. When you think you've come up with the answers, you're going to write them down. Next, you're going to ask her to do the same. And then you will put your noodles together, compare notes, and draft a blueprint for a great relationship.

Did you notice two key words?

Draft. Like you (and her), this is a work in progress. As you both evolve over time, you will revisit your blueprint, together.

Blueprint. Think of it as a high-level game plan for the team of two or a map for the road trip of a lifetime. It is *not* a contract. It's so important that you both understand this, that a chapter (p. 41) is devoted to dissuading you of the folly.

About her: What makes you choose her over every other woman?

Glance through your notes from *How to Spot a Dragon* (p. 23). Did you miss anything, good, bad, or ugly? Tell her what you like. What you aren't sure about.

About you: What do you bring to the relationship? We're talking about personal qualities, not a balance sheet. Why do you think she would choose you over every other man?

About you & her, together: Why do you think some relationships work while others don't? What makes you two great? Hint: think about what your friends and family say about you as a couple. What are your life dreams as a great couple? What are your major concerns? How will you deal with them? What will you do if you win the lottery? Or lose the farm and go bankrupt? What's the best you can be together? What do you have to do to get there?

Now that you two have some basic *what* concepts figured out, it's time to throw them up against the *how* wall. This is *how* you and your Mate will live together. Because when things get messy—and they will—you'll want to be on the same playing field as your Mate. It doesn't matter *which* playing field, as long as it's the same one. You need to figure out if one of you thinks you're playing football, while the other is playing basketball.

In his book, *All I Really Need to Know I Learned in Kindergarten*, Robert Fulghum lays out some of his Golden Rules:

1. Share everything
2. Play fair
3. Don't hit people
4. Put things back where you found them
5. Clean up your own mess
6. Don't take things that aren't yours
7. Say you're sorry when you hurt someone

Here's another one to consider:

8. No public sniping (taking pot shots in front of others)

While these are not rocket science, many relationships come to an end because one of these eight little gems is violated. No one is perfect, but having a thoughtful conversation with your Mate—about sharing (finances, housework, your offspring's sleepless nights), putting things back where you found them (hello, toilet seat), playing fair, and saying sorry (and meaning it) when you screw up—is a genius move.

The devil is in the details, so get a head start and talk about your golden rules together.

Deal breakers

These are the hard-core principles that are hardwired into your DNA. Tell each other with brutal frankness where your lines are, which, if crossed, could be the end of a beautiful friendship. There are no right or wrong answers; you just need to talk—and listen—openly and respectfully.

Some conversation starters might be:

1. Infidelity
2. Being abusive, physically or emotionally (Be specific. Shouting may be cathartic for one but traumatic for the other.)
3. Addictions (Again, be specific. Wine at dinner may be cool for you but could send your partner into a tailspin after being raised by an alcoholic parent.)
4. Heinous swear words
5. Religion (a big deal for some, not so much for the rest of us)
6. Political affiliation (see #5 above)
7. Porn
8. Breaking the law / incarceration
9. Sex, i.e., what does good, giving, and game look like to each of you? (Be specific. If you

are wildly unmatched in how often and how you like sex, odds are this issue will eclipse your otherwise awesome pairing.)

This may all seem like a great idea to some and a helluva lot of work to others. Here's what I know: you can do the work now or pay later.

If you talk about this important stuff up front, you are laying the foundation for a great relationship. If you *keep* talking more than the average four minutes a day, your chances of having a great relationship—and great sex—with your Mate are going to be a lot higher than the current 50 per cent divorce rate.

DECLARATION
OF INTERDEPENDENCE

Your Declaration of Interdependence (DOI) is the epicenter of your relationship. It is the draft blueprint for you and your Mate to live happily ever after. The concept has been shamelessly lifted from a long-term super-happily married couple who call their DOI a "Magna Carta." You can call it whatever you want, as long as you have one.

This is not about prenups or marriage contracts. Those are designed by lawyers, whose purpose is to navigate the law on behalf of their clients in order to maximize the upside—or at least minimize the downside—for their client. This competitive win-lose approach is *not* the model for a great long-term relationship with your Mate.

In the spirit of gentle fun and laughter, cue the DOI. In the previous chapter you pondered some big questions, first separately and then together. You talked to each other about what you wrote, and more importantly, about what you *heard* your Mate say. You agreed on your Golden Rules and talked frankly about your Deal Breakers. Now is the time to put them in writing.

I am tempted to end the chapter here because most men *hate* writing this sort of thing, but due to popular demand from their Mates, here goes.

Firstly, here's an example of what it should *not* look like:

> *In case I should be the direct cause of a ring around the bathtub after taking a bath, I will, with the aid of Swift's Cleanser and a brush, not my washcloth, remove said ring.*

This is one of the marvelous clauses from a 1947 contract between writer Kurt Vonnegut and his wife Jane.[7]

Now here's an example of what your DOI could look like:

OUR DECLARATION OF INTERDEPENDENCE

(His and hers) I love your sexy body/bank account/car/smile/confidence.

But best of all, I love the way you make me laugh/treat me like a princess/really listen to me/bring out the best in me/clean up after yourself.

The most important thing about "us" is being best friends/saving rent on two places/being spared online dating and blind dates/great sex/becoming MMP (married, mortgaged, and parents).

Our Golden Rules are: 1) Put things back where you found them (Specifically, the toilet lid goes back down, and whoever finishes the toilet paper installs a new roll. Putting it on the floor doesn't count.); 2) The last one out of the bed has to make it; 3) Good, giving, and game (Specifically, once a week is nice, but twice a week is better, and any time we're in a new place); 4) Take turns (Specifically, if he has a boys' night out, she gets to have girls' time).

Our Deal Breakers are lies, sex with others (real or virtual), joining the Official Monster Raving Loony party, dogs that are small enough to fit inside a six-pack box, and margarine.

We promise that we will: abide by our Golden Rules and not commit Deal Breakers; let me keep my T-shirt collection; tell each other, politely but firmly, when s/he is being a Dragon or Douche; have each other's back (especially with my mother); and not cheat.

We promise to revisit this annually, or sooner if s/he is being a Dragon/Douche, and not to use the DOI as a weapon, especially when we are fighting.

Now what?

Sign and date it, and each keep a copy. Put it in a safe place. Before you fall into bed and celebrate, make a note to "revisit DOI" on your calendar in three months' time. This is ideal for a quick review; is your DOI doable or off the mark? Have another go at your draft.

Then at least annually, you're going to dust off your DOI, talk about what's working for you, what's not working, and what needs to change. Life changes us, and your relationship also needs to change in order to endure.

Congratulations! You have made your Declaration of Interdependence to each other.

ASSUME NOTHING

So you've figured out the answers to some Big Questions, and maybe you've even drafted a rockin' DOI. Just how many assumptions are buried in there, waiting for you like landmines?

One of my **un**-studies* reveals that the seeds of future *what-was-I-thinking* epiphanies are almost always present in the beginning.

[*An **un**ashamedly **un**scientific, statistically **un**reliable look at hundreds of **un**happy singles and couples.]

Start with your Deal Breakers and put them under the microscope. For example, there is no point in figuring out who takes out the garbage or picks up the dry cleaning when your understanding of, say, fidelity is light years apart. Some of us have a hard time coming to terms with the idea of having sex with just one (!) person for the rest of our lives. Actually, that may not be the struggle. We're OK with having sex with that one person forever; what we can't come to terms with is the idea of *not* having sex with *any other people* for the rest of our lives.

One married North American friend was pontificating over this at a dinner party. His argument was that the French understood that love and sex were two different things. A Frenchman could love his wife passionately and be happily married to her, yet, with her knowledge, have sex with other women. He was enthusiastic in his praise for the French. His wife deadpanned, "That's nice, but we don't live in France."

What does fidelity mean to you? To her? What if you slept with another woman? If she slept with another man? Under what circumstances would it ever be justified? What about threesomes? Before you get all excited, consider the *other* kind of threesome, where you invite another man into your bed. Remember, good, giving, and game cuts both ways.

Couples misjudge each other's understanding of sexual exclusivity. A 2011 study of 434 young heterosexual couples ages 18–25 found that, in almost half of the couples, only one partner said the couple agreed to be monogamous. The other partner said *there was no agreement.*[8] Oops.

What about kids? Do you want to have any? When? How many? Kids are a full-time job. Who is going to take that on? Even if you win the parenting trifecta with doting grandparents, a fantastic nanny, and one of you stays home full time, after you've each put in a 10-hour day at your respective "jobs," how are you going to share kid duty?

Even if you don't want kids, when your Mate gets a killer promotion that doubles your household income but requires her to travel every other week or to live in a different city, how will that work?

If you think you know her answers to these questions, you are not only wrong, you're completely clueless. Not only do you *not* know what she is truly thinking, but you rarely will. She will confound you at every turn. But that doesn't give you license to shrug your shoulders and hope for the best. Take the lead on this. Unless she is a Dragon, she will appreciate your leadership and meet you more than halfway in these thoughtful conversations.

Not sure where to start? Try your Deal Breakers (p. 33). Ask those awkward questions and *listen* for the rationale behind her words. Dig deep, asking *why is that* several times. By the time you get to the fourth or fifth *why*, you're starting to get to the real heart of the issue—and to her heart.

NOT A CONTRACT

Your DOI reflects a fixed point in time when you and your Mate did three things: you talked about what was important to you, you agreed on what mattered, and you wrote it down.

But guess what? Stuff happens. People change. Just because something worked beautifully way back when or even yesterday, there are no guarantees that it will work today or tomorrow.

Your DOI is like you, a work in progress. Remember the key words *draft* and *blueprint?* It is OK to fine-tune your DOI from time to time because it's not a contract. In fact, fine-tuning is more than OK; regular tinkering is highly recommended. You wouldn't skip the 10,000-mile service on your awesome new car, so why would you skip maintenance on your awesome new relationship? Gently polishing up your DOI is a trigger for you and your Mate to turn toward each other strategically on a regular basis.

But—lawyers and engineers please take note— your DOI is an agreement in principle, *not* a contract. It is neither enforceable nor is it binding. You are relying on the reputation and willingness of two people to make it work. And that means it is not OK to use your DOI as a weapon with which to bludgeon each other when you're pissed off or fighting, with one exception which I'll come back to.

For example, when she won't let you have sex for *forever* because you forgot her birthday. Or when she left her hair clogging the shower drain. Again. If you're fighting because one of you is ignoring your Golden Rules, don't blame your DOI. The answer doesn't lie with it; the answer lies with whichever one of you is acting like a five-year-old. Grow up. Stop being a Douche / Dragon and disrespecting your Mate (and yourself). Take a look at *The Gripe List* (p. 105) if you need help in dealing with the small stuff.

However, if you're fighting because one of you is ignoring your DOI, stop the play and throw down the red flag immediately. Both of you need to sit down without fireworks and understand what is changing and *why*.

For example, you may want a career change, which is not unreasonable in itself. According to the U.S. Department of Labor, the average worker will change careers three to five times. But if you want to switch from earning big bucks and living in a major city to being a market gardener and living in Hicksville, your way of life will undergo a seismic shift. Your Mate may have more than a little to say about that.

As for the one exception that might entitle you to bludgeon (or be bludgeoned by) your Mate with your DOI, think about your Deal Breakers. For example, monogamy may be so fundamentally important to you that it is sacrosanct. If she cheats, it's over.

Your job is to take the lead on your DOI so that you and your Mate have the best chance of changing *together*, not apart. It may be irresolvable if your fundamental principles cannot be honored by your

Mate or vice versa, but you'll only find out if you have a respectful conversation about it. Either overhaul your DOI or walk away with dignity and grace. Don't settle; you both deserve the best relationship you can have.

GOOD THING

STEP 2

Keep a
Good Thing Going

SEVEN-MINUTE RULE

Yes, the U.S. hockey team did beat Russia in the 1980 Olympic Games. Miracles do happen. Pigs do fly.

Well, two out of three ain't bad.

Keep the magic alive with your Mate, or bring the magic back better than before, with the silver bullet of relationships: the seven-minute rule.

When you see your Mate at the end of the day, take seven minutes to give her three things:

1. **A smile**

This requires that you stop what you are doing. Put down the potato peeler or your phone, and *look* at your Mate while smiling. Remember when you couldn't take your eyes off her? If you can't remember the last time you looked at her face—*really* looked—take a moment longer to enjoy the view.

2. **A hug**

Hold her in your arms for seven seconds. Not a split second. Not an eternity. Just seven seconds. Count them—silently!—in your head. Now you have not only stopped what you are doing and looked at your Mate, but you have also walked (or skipped or run) to her and greeted her with your smile and your body.

The
MINUTE
RULE

3.   Undivided attention

Give her your undivided attention for another six minutes and fifty-three seconds. You get time off from your seven minutes for the hug. Accountants appreciate not double counting.

This is not your opportunity to offload about the moron who cut you off in traffic, the brutal meeting you had with your boss, or the kids' endless fighting. The sole purpose of the seven-minute rule is to make your Mate the center of your attention for perhaps the only time all day that she has had that privilege.

Your Mate may find your behavior strange and—God forbid—pull away and look at you quizzically, but don't fold! Keep smiling, keep your hands on her arms or shoulder or whatever part of her anatomy *she* likes you to touch, and keep your focus on her for seven minutes.

If seven minutes feels like an eternity, you're out of practice like a golf swing in winter. Stay the course. You deserve better than the average guy who spends a paltry four minutes a day alone, uninterrupted with his partner. Mr. Average spends longer than that on the can!

Not sure what to talk about? Try some of these:

"How did your day treat you, sweetheart?"

"How did your (very important meeting/sales pitch/presentation/interview go)?"

"Tell me, beautiful, what was the best part of your day?"

"Did you get to talk to _____ about ____?"

"Honey, how is your new (secretary/assistant/boss) working out?"

If your Mate had a lousy day, ask the magic question, "What can I do to help you?" And then *listen*. Do not attempt to "fix" her day or solve her problems. She simply needs to blow off steam. If this is a revelation to you, fast forward to *She Is Not a Toaster* (p. 72).

If your Mate asks you to do something ("Can you take care of dinner tonight? I have to read a report."), *do it right away* and *do not ask for instructions* on how to do it. The hardest part of making dinner is figuring out what to make. When your Mate says, "Can you take care of dinner?" she means: "Figure out what to have for dinner, and then make it."

Don't expect that your Mate will reciprocate immediately. Lavish the seven-minute rule on her for a week or two before you suggest that you'd like to tell her about your day—always *after* you've asked her about her day first.

Did you notice something? Now you're up to 14 minutes! Congratulations. You're almost halfway to the magic 30 minutes a day and on your way to being a *great* guy in a *great* relationship. You deserve this great relationship. Go for it!

A note to parents with ankle biters, otherwise known as kids and pets: *ignore them*. They are greedy and insatiable and can get your undivided attention for the rest of the evening. Give your Mate her seven little minutes and vice versa, for crying out loud. And the ankle biters *will* cry out loud. Set the kitchen timer if you have to, and tell them to leave you alone unless there are flames or blood. As you show them what a great couple looks like, they will thrive in the glow of you and your Mate's new bliss.

DO IT NOW,
DO IT FOREVER

Whether you are a Diamond or a Douche, you're typically on your best behavior when you're courting. Most men work hard at wooing a woman they want to impress. You open the car door for her. You call or text if you're running more than a few minutes late. You tell her she looks gorgeous. You try out those hair product samples shoved in the back of the bathroom drawer. You step up your gym workouts or at least think about it. You bring her flowers and fill her wineglass. You bring her a morning coffee when she stays over.

This is the considerate man she falls in love with. You earn her affection, her trust, her sex, and ultimately, her love and respect. You and your Mate have a good thing. Well done.

But your good thing will fizzle out faster than a dollar-store sparkler if you don't *keep* your good thing going. Let's be absolutely clear about this: it is *your* job to take the lead and keep being the considerate man she fell in love with.

Whatever you did for her when you wooed her, you need to keep doing it *forever*.

Keep opening the car door for her, dressing like a stylin' guy, filling her wineglass, and telling her she is beautiful. Anything less than your courting ways is a bait and switch.

The curious thing about bait and switch is that it echoes. If you get lazy, you give licence to your Mate to do the same.

Fortunately, the opposite is also true. When a woman feels that her Mate appreciates her, she usually appreciates him back. You give her an arsenal of treasures to flaunt at her girlfriends when they're whining about their lazy-assed Mates who don't appreciate their women. Showing off her fabulously considerate guy makes your Mate happier than when she's buying a new pair of shoes.

One of my friends is a very Australian male. He grew up in the outback, works on cattle stations, and cuts off calf testicles as easily as shelling peas. You don't get more "typical Aussie bloke" than that. He and his Mate have been married for over 30 years and have three great grown-up kids. At a family event, the conversation turned to what makes marriages work or fail. When pushed for an answer as to what made his marriage work for three decades, he conceded that he made his Mate a cup of morning coffee, milk with two sugars. There was a moment of silence while this was digested, then a flurry of voices insisting that there must be more to a successful marriage than that. He replied, "If you bring her a cup of coffee in the beginning, you bring her a cup of coffee forever. Simple."

Other friends who are going strong after 20-plus years are on different schedules. He's the early bird lawyer out the door at 5:30 a.m., whereas she's the night owl homemaker who is traumatized by any hour before 8:00 a.m. Being a smart man, he quietly makes his coffee to go and slips away without disturbing his sleeping wife. On the kitchen counter, he leaves for her "her" teacup with a particular tea bag, one sugar inside, and a full kettle of water ready for her to push the "on" button when she stumbles out of bed hours later.

When I was their houseguest and saw this ritual every morning, I asked my hosts about it. They were nonplussed. It was no big deal; he'd done it "forever" for her.

Here's his formula:

(SIMPLE ACTS OF THOUGHTFULNESS)
X (CONSISTENTLY DELIVERED)
= HAPPY MATE

LOWER HER EXPECTATIONS

It's 6:00 p.m. You reach for your jacket and keys and head for the office door. You are pleased with yourself, since you've had a great day's work, and for the first time this week, you're going to be home on time. Your boss intercepts you with the news that your most important client has a crisis. A real one. It needs to be handled *yesterday*; tomorrow is too late. Your company's reputation and cash flow are at stake. The client represents a big slice of your company's revenue. A few questions ascertain that the problem is fixable, and that you are the right guy to fix it. If you push hard, you could be out of the office by 8:00 p.m.

The only problem is that you promised your Mate you would be home for dinner tonight. It has been on the calendar for months. Her parents are in town overnight on a rare visit, and you have son-in-law obligations to fulfill.

You call her and say, "Honey, I'm sorry. I have bad news. I need to work late tonight on the Most Important Client file. Probably until about 9:00 or 9:30, but I'll really hit it hard and see if I can get it done a little earlier. Please apologize to your parents for me. I will join you for dessert and coffee, and drive them to their hotel afterward."

When you walk in the door at 8:15 p.m., you are a star. Although your initial news disappointed her, you had the backbone to handle it.

On the flip side, if you weasel out of dinner with the vague promise that you need to stay at work "a little late, hopefully I'll be done by 7:00," you've disappointed her twice.

N-E-V-E-R CRITICIZE

The best wedding gift that Steve received was from his long-time family doctor, an old school gentleman. As the happy couple made their way around to guests at the reception, the elegant doctor quietly slipped a note into Steve's pocket. "This is the secret to a long and happy marriage," he whispered as he warmly clasped the new husband's hand in congratulations.

The beautiful notepaper had four words handwritten on it:

NEVER CRITICIZE YOUR WIFE

Glorious advice...which Steve has not always followed. Compounding his error, Steve has moments of blistering stupidity when he not only criticizes his Mate, but then shoots himself in his other testicle with rigorously accurate facts demonstrating how *he is right* and she is wrong. And then Steve wonders why their sex life has evaporated.

"But my wife *is* wrong sometimes. I let the small stuff slide, but sometimes it's big stuff. Like the time she got into a fender bender because she was distracted by the dog/kids/cell phone." Or when she forgot the kids at the grocery store.

You're entitled to complain. "I'm angry that you borrowed my car yesterday and left it empty. I was late for my first appointment, because I had to stop and fill it."

But you are not entitled to criticize. "You're so thoughtless. Once again, you borrowed my car and left it empty. I'm fed up with looking like an idiot when I rush in late to work."

Take charge of this; it's *your* job to lead. You have a choice: you can lead to a crappy place where you get your moment of satisfaction by criticizing her, followed by your much longer days or weeks of purgatory when she freezes your ass out of the bedroom...or you can take the high road and give her *feedback*. This is not a new age euphemism for criticism; it's a different beast entirely.

Imagine for a moment that you are chairman of the board of a successful international organization. One of your fellow directors has screwed up. Big time. Nothing malicious, simply an error of judgment that shouldn't have happened. How are you going to handle this? Do you wait until the end of a long day and ambush him with accusations and recriminations, telling him how careless/stupid/ wrong he is and how pissed off you are?

Or do you make time to talk with him when you're both focused and alert, and you calmly lay out the situation as you understand it then ask for his view of the situation. He is probably mortified that the situation occurred and grateful for a chance to deconstruct his screw-up to someone who is calm and in control. You talk together about what could have been done to prevent it from happening, and what needs to be done to make it right and to prevent it from happening again.

You ask the magic question: "What can I do to help?" Together you generate options that you work through and decide upon. He is grateful to you for the masterful way you have tackled this situation, and you have earned yourself a loyal colleague whose respect for you has gone through the roof.

So the next time you think your Mate has effed up, bring some of that CEO touch home with you. Avoid the trap of being your best self with your coworkers and giving only your tired, less-than-awesome self to your Mate. Never criticize and you will earn yourself a loyal Mate who deeply respects you and has your back.

CHIVALRY IS SEXY

Let's be perfectly clear: chivalry is *sexy*. Good manners are appreciated by women of all ages, not just your grandma.

Precisely what defines good manners can vary around the edges depending on your vintage, but the basics—the substantial core of good manners—never go out of fashion. The basics include: *please* and *thank you*; being on time; holding the door to let her pass through; listening (not merely pretending to listen); offering her your jacket when the weather is chilly; filling her plate and glass first; insisting she have the last chocolate/splash of wine/whatever; rising to greet her when she comes home; helping to bring stuff in from the car *without being asked*; and eating with your mouth shut.

This is not the stuff of courtship. If you want to keep your good thing going, these simple gestures need to be on automatic pilot until you die.

Kate dated a man who spent some of his growing-up years in the southern U.S. He had outstanding manners. "Yes, ma'am" or "No, ma'am" to shop assistants, offering her the first helping at dinner, filling her wineglass, a moonlit picnic, and even sliding her chair underneath her when she sat down. It was like being in an elegant movie where women glided on the arms of suave gentlemen.

This behavior continued for a few months until one day as Mr. Southern was holding open the car door for her, Kate commented on how much she appreciated his good manners. He grinned and confessed that he only opened car doors at the start, to impress a woman, and then she would be on her own. Kate grinned in return and told Mr. Southern that manners were not only important to her, but his old school manners were one of the reasons she was attracted to him. Mr. Southern was either obtuse or not that into her, because he never opened a car door for Kate again. It turned out that opening doors was one of many of Mr. Southern's wooing tactics that were short lived. His bait-and-switch strategy was revealed: lateness, half-assed excuses, tattered underwear, unimaginative dates, and the unforgivable sin of never remembering Kate's son's name. Shortly thereafter, Mr. Southern became Mr. Single again.

A bit harsh? If your response is along these lines, ask yourself how your current level of manners is working for you. Are you attracting Diamonds? Do they stick around? Hmmm, not so much? Maybe the guy in the mirror needs a manners makeover.

But, you say, my Mate doesn't like me holding the door for her. She's a feminist and says it's patronizing. I say two things. Firstly, your Mate is confusing manners (the glue that holds civilization together) with fairness (equal pay and opportunity). Sincere good manners are gestures of consideration, not put-downs. Of course, women are perfectly capable of hauling their bags off the luggage carousel, but if a man is present—sons included—their good manners kick in and they grab the bags. If several bags come together and he can't possibly grab them at once, well-mannered women don't watch helplessly. They will grab the lighter bag(s) as a show of *their* good manners.

Secondly, it might not be her, it might be *you*. Are you naturally good mannered, at ease with opening doors and taking her bags? Just like your golf swing, these things take practice. Choose one gesture that you want to perfect, say, opening the door for women, and practice that diligently for a month. You'll be a pro in no time, and women will be impressed by that much more than they will be impressed by your golf swing.

A special word for the dads: good manners are even more important if you have kids. You are showing your sons to respect women, and you are showing your daughters to *expect* respect from men. My kids complained about our relentless insistence on good manners. Of course, we were the only parents on the planet with a manners obsession. Our kids whined ceaselessly that none of their friends' parents chastised them for talking with their mouths full or made them write thank-you notes to distant relatives after birthdays. But once my kids hit their teens, they started to notice things. "OMG, dinner at my friend's house last night was heinous. The whole family talks with food coming out of their mouths. They're so rude. And their mom did all the cooking and no one helped or said thank-you." As young adults, my kids are irrevocably turned off by bad manners. "She's always late and full of lame excuses.

I'm not putting up with that crap." Or, "I'm not going out with someone who eats like a pig. Ewww."

And now a special word for the guys who have chivalrously sexy manners and can't find a woman who appreciates them: keep the faith. She's out there somewhere and worth waiting for.

BACK SUPPORT

There *is* a magic ingredient for a great, long-term relationship with your Mate. Forget the guesswork, the shopping list, and especially the compatibility promises of your mother and online dating sites. Turn off your phone, close the door, and bring your full attention to this page as the secret is revealed.

Through another **un**-study, I have learned that one of the most important ingredients for an enduring relationship is being able to answer "YES!" unequivocally to the question, "Do you have each other's backs?"

What does this mean?

Your Mate is your champion and defender. You know that she will *always* back you in public. Your friends and family see the warm and respectful way that you speak to—and about—each other, and they appreciate being part of the circle of two people who have their act together.

Here is where it gets interesting. Most people *think* they have their Mate's back, but they do or say things that are the *opposite*. Pot shots in public are often a speciality.

"Mate has been super busy, but she loves her work. She loves it so much that she brought it along on our getaway weekend to Dreamyville last month." (Criticism and sarcasm)

"We're focusing on my career because Mate only has a college diploma. Don't you, sweetheart?" (Contempt)

"I'm surprised that Mate signed up for the charity fun run. She's not a fan of exercise, but she is a fan of the couch." (Sarcasm)

"Wow, Mate is the soccer team's treasurer? Watch out. She spends money like water. Just as well I'm here to balance the checkbook." (Criticism and contempt)

So what *does* back support look like?

Your best friend who can't stand your Mate: What is the big deal? If you love them both, keep them apart and insist on no trash talking. In a healthy relationship, you have your friends, your Mate has her friends, and you both have friends together.

The family gathering: Your mother does the old snide-comment-behind-the-veil-of-sweetness trick on your Mate. No matter how annoying your Mate may find your mom, you have universal sympathy for being in a no-win situation. WTF to do? Instead of pretending you are deaf, politely but firmly tell your mother that your Mate is the love of your life and to knock it off. You do this even though you know your Mate is more than capable of handling mother dearest herself.

The kid/s: Read the seven-minute rule (p. 47). Tell your kids about it, give them the shocking news that your Mate comes first, and stick to it. Your Mate gets the first seven minutes. If the kids ask nicely, they can get the next seven minutes—*after* your Mate.

Once kids are upright, they will try to manipulate one parent against the other until the end of time.

This is normal; it's part of their job description. If your Mate has made a decision, you must support it in front of your kid(s). If you want to disagree with her, do it in a way that (i) shows you have her back, and (ii) shows your kids how to fight fair (p. 99).

Give your Mate unequivocal back support and ask for the same. You're standing taller already, and it looks damn good.

WHY LISTENING GETS YOU LAID

Relationship therapists and marriage counselors who promote communication, communication, and more communication as the key to improving your relationship have the wrong end of the stick, according to Dr. John Gottman and a team of psychologists at Seattle's University of Washington.[9] Men complain that women talk too much, yet therapists encourage *more* of the very thing that is driving you nuts.

There are (unsubstantiated) reports floating around that women use approximately 10,000 words each day compared to a man's 7,000 words.[10] The exact numbers vary depending on which "report" you read, but the concept is the same: women out-talk men by a substantial factor. Why? Because women have to repeat everything!

If you want your Mate to put her daily word count on a diet, try two simple techniques:

1. Listen the *first* time; and
2. *Ask* ass-saving questions.

More on this later. First, let's understand why listening gets you laid.

The act of listening requires you to *turn toward each other*. Gottman's research shows that happily married couples connect with and acknowledge each other often.[11] While you might think that romantic getaways will put your Mate in the mood for love, analysis shows that it's the abundance of simple exchanges about the humdrum stuff of life that keep her turned toward you.

What do these simple exhanges look like? Send her a text message saying that you hope her presentation went well or to thank her for dropping you off at the airport and you miss her already. Or check in with her:

"Sweetie, I'm heading to the store. Would you like me to pick up the dry cleaning?"

"Hey beautiful, did you meet that new golf pro at the club this morning?"

"Honey, how's that book you're reading?"

With unhappy couples, your Mate doesn't bother to look up from her book, and you don't even notice. The small but vital moments of connection with your Mate are rare, and the pilot light of your relationship wanes.

However if you keep your pilot light burning by staying in touch with everyday interactions, the small annoyances will slide past with less drama and your romantic flourishes will turn up the heat. Keep yourself turned toward your Mate, and she will be less likely to turn her back on you in bed.

BEING RIGHT MAKES YOU DEAF

Being right is important. We want engineers to be right when they design a bridge or an airplane. We want our laser surgeon to be right when s/he points a red beam onto our eyeballs. We want the drive-thru kid to be right when s/he fills our order.

But being right makes you deaf. Most couples suffer in the hearing department. They go from rose-colored hearing aids to a state of deafness in a devastatingly fast trajectory.

There is an avalanche of information on how to improve your listening skills. Active listening, validation, embodied empathy, and so on. You could study for years and write an outstanding thesis. But research shows that only 35 per cent of couples see a meaningful improvement in their marriages as a result of the therapy.[12] The reason why active listening doesn't work well for *couples* is that the person "listening" is not an impartial third party; s/he is the person who is being lambasted. It takes the emotional intelligence of a superhero to deal with someone trashing you.

One of the startling research findings is that "most couples who have maintained happy marriages rarely do anything that even partly resembles active listening when they're upset."[13]

Nonetheless, listening takes up 45 per cent of our time spent communicating,[14] so it's worth finding ways to do it better, both with your Mate when she's *not* upset and also with every other person in your orbit. (The rest of our communication time is spent speaking at 30 per cent, reading at 16 per cent, and writing at 9 per cent.)

My favorite approach—the one that saves my ass every time—identifies *three* ways to listen. The two that we use most often *do not work*. They are:

1. We agree

"I am hearing you. What you are saying is consistent with what I know to be true. The information is right, and so you are right, because I am right. I don't even really need to hear you anymore, so let's move on."

2. We disagree

"I am hearing you, but it is inconsistent with what I know to be true. One of us is wrong, and it isn't me. I can't even hear you anymore because I am busy working on my rebuttal to show how wrong you are."

When we come from these two ways of listening—agreeing or disagreeing—no *new information* ever gets in. If you're always right, then everything is always in agreement with what you know to be true or untrue.

If nothing new is coming at you, it means you shall remain the same. And when things change around you, say, when your rose-colored hearing aid shuts off and you become deaf, men are stuck in the unhappy trade-off of being right and pissing off their Mate, and women mistake men's compliance for being heard.

Enter the third way of listening. The one that works.

3. Allow yourself to be curious about what the other person is saying. There are no *agree* or *disagree* boxes to check with your mental pen, just information that you are allowing yourself to be curious about.

The third way of listening sounds like this:

"Hmmm, I never thought about it that way before. Tell me more."

"I'm not sure I follow you. Run it by me again?"

"That's interesting! How would that work?"

Or my all-time favorite:

"Oh, that's interesting. Why would you say that?"

Note: your tone is crucial; sarcasm or contempt are toxic.

If you find yourself blaming or finding fault with the information, you are no longer letting it in. Allow yourself to hear things that aren't being said, i.e., the idea *underneath* the words. *Now* you're starting to communicate with each other.

You may feel awkward at first and it might not come easily, but persistence will take your relationship to a great place. The third way of listening is like golf or sex: it's a skill which needs to be consciously practiced and honed to get better.

The coolest thing about listening the third way is that your conversations pivot in a new direction. Instead of heading down the why-don't-you-ever-listen path, you are drawing out your Mate in the same way you did when you were getting to know her. She fell in love with you then. When you listen the third way, she is reminded why she fell in love with such an awesome guy.

SHE IS NOT A TOASTER

Men love to fix things. They diagnose the problem, come up with a solution, and connect the two with the straightest line possible. This efficient approach almost always works just fine for mechanical things, say, a toaster or a flat tire, and you will earn brownie points from your Mate who just wants the damn thing fixed.

It's reasonable to assume that you are also well skilled at fixing things and solving problems at work, whether you are tracing an electrical fault to its source or removing brain tumors. "Yes," you nod, "I'm pretty good at slicing out those pesky astrocytomas."

Slow down a moment. Just because you're a whiz at problem solving in your garage or workplace, it will go badly for you to try to problem solve for your Mate. This is a universally common experience for men. *If you take only one idea from this book, let it be this one.*

When you come home and she immediately starts complaining about something DO NOT UNDER ANY CIRCUMSTANCES TRY TO HELP BY SOLVING HER PROBLEM.

One of my emotionally intelligent male friends who has been mostly happily married for over 20 years told me this was "an absolute revelation" to him. His Mate had already told him to "quit being a lawyer," but he didn't really get it until he heard the advice from someone else. He now gives this advice, unsolicited, to every young guy in the office when he hears the guy's moving in with his Mate or getting married.

So what *do* you do when she bursts through the door ranting furiously about her idiot carpool passenger/incompetent boss/rude grocery store clerk? As instinctive and tempting as it is to hightail it in the opposite direction, try this instead.

1. Ask her, "Honey, tell me what happened?" and listen. Under no circumstances do you *pretend* to listen, because that will immediately channel her fury into your head. Turn off the stove, hit "record" on your DVR, give her your full attention, and *listen*.

2. Take her side. Instead of saying, "Well, why don't you just drive by yourself next time so you won't have to listen to him," you say, "I can't believe he said that to you. What an ass! How did you manage not to wallop his stupid head with your purse?"

If you're good—really good—you might make gentle offerings of sympathy. "You poor thing. What happened next? What did everyone else have to say?" And keep listening.

3. When you think she might be running out of steam, and if—*only if*—there is a strong chance that your Mate might benefit from your assistance, ask her with absolute sincerity, "Beautiful, what can I do to help you?" Tone is *crucial*. Again, don't give her a reason to turn her firehose on you.

If your Mate takes you up on your offer of help— maybe she suggests that you secretly buy out her company and fire the idiot carpooler/incompetent boss, or that you pummel the grocery store clerk with stale donuts—then you're on your merry problem-solving way. Remember to stay wingman and follow her lead.

If she doesn't take you up on your offer, sit back and continue to listen. She may stomp off to another room, slam doors, bang pots around the kitchen, whatever. Resist the urge to follow her, unless she's crying. Turning a blind eye to a distressed and crying woman is clueless *and* heartless. Be her hero and give her back support. Take her a box of tissues, gently place a reassuring hand on her shoulder or back (not on her ass), sit, and listen.

It will pass.

And if it doesn't pass? I've got you covered: fast forward to *Read The Subtitles* (p. 134).

ASS-SAVING QUESTIONS

The best experts in their field are highly skilled at asking questions, even stupid ones. From kindergarten students to Nobel Prize-winning scientists, it is their questions as much as—or, perhaps, more than—their answers that have pushed them ahead of their peers. They ask *real* questions, not statements disguised as questions.

Asking questions is not always a comfortable role for men. My theory is that an aversion to asking questions is part of the fixation of "being right." Asking genuine questions says "I don't know." If you don't know something, you can't be right. The opposite of "I don't know" is being right, i.e., whipping out answers and solutions faster than a gunslinger. This approach may hold in situations at work or while playing sports, but things will go badly if whipping out answers and solutions is the default approach you take to your Mate.

However, it will also go badly if the questions you ask are clueless. All the brownie points you earn by refraining from fixing your Mate's issues, and instead listening to her, will now blow up in your face if you inadvertently ask the wrong questions. The same thing will happen if you misuse questions to make a statement ("Wasn't your sister rude tonight?") or to trap your Mate into a difficult position ("If you really cared about me, you would try harder to get along with my mom.")

So when you are following the seven-minute rule and you ask your Mate, "How was your day, honey?" and her firehose of fury is unleashed upon your unsuspecting head, here is the cheat sheet of questions that will save you.

1. "**W**ho … /what/where/when?" *(facts)*
2. "**W**hat … happened next?" *(details & consequences)*
3. "**W**hen … (the above) happened, what do you think caused it?" *(source or cause)*
4. "**W**here… did it go next?" or "What did that cause/create?" *(details and consequences)*
5. "**W**hy do you think that happened? What were you expecting?" *(unmet expectations)*
6. "**H**ow … would you prefer things to be/happen?" *(future possibilities)*

(Hard to remember? Mediators sometimes file these into memory as "The Five **W**ives and **H**enry.")

As you try to commit these to your memory, stand back and take a big picture view of the questions. The first four questions are intended to explore *past and present* behaviors, consequences/impacts, and assumptions. These need to be explored thoroughly before the conversation shifts to the *future* with the last two questions: unmet expectations and positions versus interests.

Ass-saving questions are the building blocks of great relationships, resolving conflict and overcoming resistance. Be patient; this may be a whole new way of talking for you and your Mate, and a new way of turning toward each other.

HOW'S THAT WORKING FOR YOU?

Now that you've mastered the third way of listening and you know the difference between your Mate and a toaster, what do you do when your otherwise happy Mate has a beef that she won't let go? Something keeps bugging her and interrupting your happiness. You have clarified with her that it's *not* about you (or her), rather it's about someone or something else. For example, maybe she's preoccupied with a difficult coworker or the price of potatoes. That's good news for you, sort of. But it doesn't help your deep well of patience, which may be in imminent danger of running dry.

Even worse, the solution is obvious to you and maybe even to others around her, but your otherwise wonderful Mate has developed a blind spot for this particular issue.

Next time she starts up on her favorite beef, wait patiently for an opportunity to ask her the simple question, "How's that working for you, honey?"

You may get a quizzical "huh?" in response. This is your cue to step in and invite your Mate to step *outside* her beef and look at it differently.

"Honey, you've been talking (Note: *never* use the word complaining!) about your coworker/the price of potatoes for some time, and it seems to be really upsetting you. You know I have your back on this, right? I'm not sure that your coworker/the price of potatoes is going to change any time soon. How is that working for you?"

Your purpose is to gently shift your Mate's thinking from the past and present to the future. If you skillfully ask the right questions, you're opening up the opportunity for your Mate to come up with the answers.

Donna had been plagued by pain in her right foot for years. She had developed bunions—over one in three people suffer from this cruel affliction—and despite podiatrists, orthotics, prescribed shoes, and a 10-minute morning ritual of padding and wrapping her right foot, said foot continued to torment her and to worsen. The next step was surgery, but it required her to be couch bound for a month, and full recovery would take three to four months. Donna was the poster child for women's hockey and was headed for the ranks of professional golf, and there was no window between the two sports to schedule a four-month hiatus.

As an athlete, there was a lot at stake for Donna. As a wife, there was also a lot at stake. David, her wonderfully supportive husband, had patiently listened to her escalating complaints for a *l-o-n-g* time. All his helpful suggestions had been dismissed or ignored by Donna, but he knew that if he dismissed or ignored Donna's complaint, he would be in the doghouse. So one evening David tried another strategy. He kept it light, chatting while they prepared dinner together.

"Donna, you've been talking about the pain in your foot for a long time, and I'm not sure that your foot is going to get better on its own any time soon. In fact, it's probably only going to get worse. How is that working for you?"

Donna responded with the customary vitriolic rant about her wretched foot. David listened and waited patiently, letting the firehose of frustration run dry.

First, David let her know that he had Donna's back. "You poor thing! I can't imagine walking around in pain all day long, much less getting around an effing golf course."

Next, David casually asked ass-saving questions to get information.

"Sweetie, who's your podiatrist?"

"Are you happy with her?"

"Great, that's good. What did she say?"

"Are there any other options?"

"Do you want to get a second opinion?"

"Wow, it sounds as though surgery is the only option for a permanent fix. Is that right?"

Once David had more information, he gently shifted their conversation from the past and present to the future.

"How long would the surgery take? What about recovery?"

"So you would be in a cast for a month, but it would be four months in total until you're back in full swing, right?"

"When can that happen?"

"Next year?! You want to stay in pain every day for another *year*?!"

"Yeah, I know you're busy looking after all of us, but beautiful, you're busy *and* cranky. That's hard on you, but do you know that it's also hard on everyone who loves you, including me."

"I understand. No, you're *not* a cranky person who hobbles around in pain; you're an awesome, happy woman and a brilliant athlete. Don't you miss her? I do, and I want her back!"

If you skillfully ask the right questions, you are opening up the opportunity for your Mate to come up with the answers.

Donna made the decision to hobble around the golf course all summer and autumn and to undergo foot surgery three weeks before Christmas. It hurt like hell for a couple of weeks, but the trade-off was that she got a free pass for all the silly holiday season events, including the annual office holiday party, which she could happily live without. From the comfort of her couch, Donna sailed through the most stress-free holiday season ever and enjoyed a full— and early—recovery. Fast forward four months. Her vibrant, fun, athletic self is back, and David is a happy guy. How's *that* working for them? Great, thank you.

ADVICE: TAKE IT
OR LEAVE IT

The blue moon rises and your Mate asks for your advice. Or at least you *think* that's what she's doing. First, make sure that she really is asking you for advice, and not simply posing a rhetorical question, which if you respond to with answers and solutions, will cause her unhappiness to not only magnify but to redirect it onto you.

If your Mate asks something along the lines of, "What do you think?" or "Don't you think?," she is *not* asking for your advice. You are a sounding board, not an advisory board. Your response to these questions should be to ask questions in return—see *Ass-Saving Questions* (p. 75).

Until she says the words, "I don't know what to do."

And then you say, cautiously, "Do you want to know what I would do?"

If she says "yes," then now you have been granted permission to give her the advice you've been busting to give all along.

So tell your Mate what you would do, and *stop talking*. Let her take it or leave it. That's it. Finito. Mission accomplished.

STEP 3

Dodge Minefields

THE MINEFIELD OF COMMUNICATION: CAN WE TALK?

Your Mate wants to get something off her chest. It may be about you, but it could also be a problem at work, with the kids, or new bathroom tiles. Your Mate is giving you the courtesy of letting you know that she needs your undivided attention.

An open attitude on your part will show your Mate that you respect her. This doesn't mean that she has you by the balls; rather, it means that you are conveying respect, not resistance.

She asks the dreaded question, "Can we talk?"

You smile and say, "Of course, gorgeous. I'll be finished with…(*whatever you're doing*)…in 20 minutes. Will that work for you?" or "Great. How about I open a bottle of wine and meet you in the living room?"

In 15 minutes time (not the 20 minutes you asked for—be early!) you head for the living room with two glasses of wine, turn down the lights, put on some mellow music, and wait for her.

Whatever she wants to talk about will be sweeter (or at least less fraught) if you're treating this occasion as if you're on a date. Hand her a glass of wine with a smile then wait for her to start. You're off to a flying start.

THE MINEFIELD OF CRAZY QUESTIONS (THAT EVEN SANE WOMEN ASK)

The people with the greatest capacity to drive you insane are the ones you love most. Your Mate tops that list. She knows how to inflict death by 1,000 paper cuts. Often, she starts out with a seemingly innocuous question which is really a crazy question in disguise. As she smiles and poses her question, you realize with a figurative slap to the forehead that you're about to get caught by her hook and reeled into the doghouse.

Here are my top crazy questions that women ask, along with genius responses that will keep you out of the doghouse.

What are you thinking?

When your Mate asks you this, she is letting you know that she wants to talk—about anything—and preferably with you. Talking is one of the most powerful ways to help women reduce stress and feel good. When a woman is relating to and connecting with someone, a chemical reaction is taking place in her body. Oxytocin is being released, evoking feelings of contentment, reductions in anxiety, and feelings of calmness and security in her. Think of oxytocin as the magic portal to surviving women.

So next time your Mate asks, "What are you thinking?" turn off your screen, turn toward her with a smile and your full attention, and say:

"Not much, beautiful. But I'd love to know what you're thinking." Or…

"I was thinking about work/the hockey game/whatever, but I'd rather be talking with you. What are you thinking about, gorgeous?"

If your Mate asks you this question *after* sex, she wants to connect (more) with you. Have some playful fun with her by saying,

"Thinking? I'm not capable of thinking; my brain just detonated. For the first time all day, I'm not thinking about how much I want to make love to the sexiest woman on the planet. Because she's right here beside me."

Do these pants make my ass look fat?

There should be a law against women asking this question or variations thereof:

"How do I look in this?"

"Do you think this bathing suit is OK?"

This is not the time for the truth; a woman who asks this type of question cannot handle the truth. Yes, those pants make her ass look fat, because she is 10 pounds heavier than when she bought them, and *she knows this* because she stepped on the scale this morning. No, that bathing suit is not OK, because it belongs on her grandmother (or on your daughter).

To stay out of trouble, do *not* answer the question. Your Mate doesn't want you to. All she wants to know is if she is still attractive to you. Your genius response is to reassure her:

"Sweetie, you look great! Every time I look at you, I see the beautiful woman who walked down the aisle to marry me." Or…

"I'm going to spend all day thinking about taking those pants off your gorgeous ass."

Do you notice anything different (about me/my hair)?

This question is brutal. I suggest you respond with,

"Honey, asking me that question is like me asking you to look at the car engine/stock exchange report/pathology analysis/whatever and asking if you notice anything different. Help me out; what awesome new thing is going on with you?"

When she says, "Babe, I just had my hair cut/colored/bought a new dress/new boobs/lost weight/whatever," you get to say: "Great! You always look great! Tell me about it, beautiful."

Encourage her to talk about the new thing, and you're off the hook.

Do you think I look old?

"Darling, what's bothering you?" accompanied by a smile and hugs.

Do you think that woman is prettier than me?

This is a no-brainer. Your genius response is, "What woman?"

Which one of my friends would you sleep with? Really, I want to know.

While you have already slept with all her friends (and her sisters) in your imagination, under no circumstances should you admit to this. And no, this is not her subtle way of letting you know she'd like a threesome. If she wants one, she will tell you.

The genius response is, "Why would I ever want to sleep with another woman when I have you?"

Do you love me?

"Yes. You are the perfect woman. I love you, and I love being with you."

THE MINEFIELD
OF GIFT GIVING

Taking the time to figure out a gift that will dazzle your Mate with your thoughtfulness is a worthy pursuit. There is no middle ground; in a woman's eyes, your gift is either awesome or lame. If you nail the art of gift giving, her respect for you will shoot sky high, and she will sing your praises to the world. If you get it wrong, you will be in the doghouse for a long time.

Your IQ won't help you, because it's not about using your noggin; it's about using your ears and that thing in your pocket. Not *that* thing, the other thing. Your cell phone. More specifically, its camera. The real reason why cell phones have a camera is about to be revealed. No, it's not for posting real-time photos of you doing party tricks.

Your phone turns two chores—buying gifts and shopping—into a treasure hunt. When you go shopping with your Mate and she says, "Oh, isn't that lovely," take a photo of said lovely thing. You don't need to go all secret spy on her; she'll figure out in a heartbeat what you're doing (even if she pretends not to). Say nothing, just smile, and take a photo.

Every time she says, "Oh, isn't that lovely," whip out your phone and go click. When she *really* likes something, she will say, "Oh, this is *really* lovely!" Pay attention. She's telling you that she wants this more than the other things you've taken photos of. And if you're slow off the mark one day because you haven't had your triple shot bucket of coffee yet, she will pointedly ask you if you brought your phone along.

Here's how it all comes together: you merrily take photos all year, every time you go shopping. *Not* just a couple of days before her special day. A month in advance, you analyze the photos you've amassed. Look for themes (jewelry? shoes? a romantic getaway?), narrow it down to a shortlist, and make your choice. If you're not sure, and if your Mate's sister/girlfriend/mother can keep a secret, ask for her input.

Order online and have it delivered to your office; don't have it delivered to your home where she might "accidentally" find it. Take the time to have the gift extravagantly wrapped, since presentation kicks the wow factor up a notch. Keep that cellphone working—order flowers to be delivered to her (at work if possible), make reservations for dinner, and you're all set.

Her big day dawns and here is where the magic begins. Wake up first, bring her the usual cup of whatever, and present her with your gift. Don't be a Douche and make her wait until the evening. Her family, friends, and coworkers are going to ask her what you gave her, so give her the pleasure of bragging about your thoughtfulness all day. They will be impressed, even more so when the flowers arrive, and your Mate's interest in having great birthday sex with her awesome man will escalate.

Now that you've got the general idea of what to do, here is a tip on what *not* to do. Never give her a gift with a plug on it. Hair dryers, vacuum cleaners, and electronic devices are not going to impress her. Even if she insists that she wants a new gizmo for her birthday and you know she will be disappointed if she doesn't get it, you need to buy her something thoughtful *as well* if you want to impress. No need to break the bank; a small gesture—scarf, theater tickets, bracelet—will go a long way. Happy birthday, beautiful.

THE MINEFIELD OF MOTHERS: #1 WOMAN IN YOUR LIFE

If you're extremely lucky, the #1 woman in your life—your mother—will be thrilled when someone special comes into your life and takes you off her hands at last. After due diligence has been carried out and the probationary period is over, your mom will graciously hand her #1 tiara to your Mate, step back from the podium wearing the #2 tiara, and you all live happily ever after.

Or not. A great deal of your future happiness is riding on this transition. If it isn't handled properly, you will suffer at the hands of the two most important women in your life, your Mate and your mother. The responsibility to dodge this Sisyphean fate rests squarely on your shoulders, so step up and show leadership early on with these two real standup women who will drive you crazy if you allow it.

Take Mom aside—perhaps dinner à deux—and thank her for raising you. Tell her she has been the #1 woman in your life and how much you appreciate what she's done for you. Then tell Mom that *her job is now done*. You appreciate her passing the baton to the new #1 woman in your life and for graciously stepping back to the #2 spot. Tell her that your heart is big enough to love them both, and you have her to thank for that.

Then tell your Mate what you told your mom, and ask her to be gracious to Mom for passing the baton.

Simple, but not always easy. What happens if, despite your awesome leadership and diplomacy, your mom and Mate whom you love with all your great big heart simply *cannot* get along?

There is no peace in fence-sitting; you must choose whose side you are on. The question to ask yourself is, "Who would you rather sleep with?"

Mothers can be subtle in their efforts to sabotage the new woman in your life. One hapless groom's parents were visiting and an evening had been set aside to celebrate. Mate pulled out all the stops to prepare a magnificent meal, the highlight of which was her specialty, cassoulet. It has been crudely described as French one-pot frank'n'beans stew, but there is nothing crude and one pot—or frank'n'beans, for that matter—about this exquisite dish. It is a canonical recipe from the South of France, in which the beans must be tarbais, the confit must be goose, and so on. The no-shortcuts version takes a *week* to prepare and is a labor of love served at the altar of only very special people.

The cassoulet is sheer perfection, the wine has been decanted, and Mom and Dad arrive, hugs and smiles all around. Mom holds you at arm's length and tells you that you've lost (or gained) weight. It doesn't matter which, if either, is true; the inference is that Mate is not taking care of you.

Mom: "Are you eating properly? Never mind, you'll eat well tonight. We're taking you to [fancy restaurant with interminable waiting list]."

You: "Wow, you got reservations at Fancy Restaurant?! That's amazing! People rave about it, but the wait list is forever. Hey honey, isn't that great?"

Mate: "Yes, that is really generous, thank you…but I thought we arranged to have dinner here. Isn't that right, sweetie? It's all ready; I've made cassoulet. It's my French grandmother's recipe, handed down from *her* grandmother."

Mom: (sniffing) "Oh, I wondered what that smell was. But we'd like to treat you to something nice. Just pop your casserole in the fridge and you can have it tomorrow night when we're gone."

Mate: "It's cassoulet, not casserole. I went to a lot of trouble preparing this. You know, first time in our new home and all that. Isn't that right, sweetie?"

You (chickenshit on the fence): "Uhhhh…"

Mom: (smiling ever so sweetly as she takes the arms of Dad and you) "That's sweet of you, dear, but these reservations won't wait. You can make your casserole for us another time. Let's go everyone. We don't want to be late."

Your mother has masterfully retained her #1 tiara, your Mate is pissed off because you didn't have her back, and your sorry ass will be frozen out of the bedroom until you fix this.

You can't take Mom's side and expect to have a 10 out of 10 relationship with your Mate. If you find yourself wavering, remind yourself who you would rather sleep with in this special circle of hell. Now go home to your #1 woman and apologize for not having her back. Nice recovery.

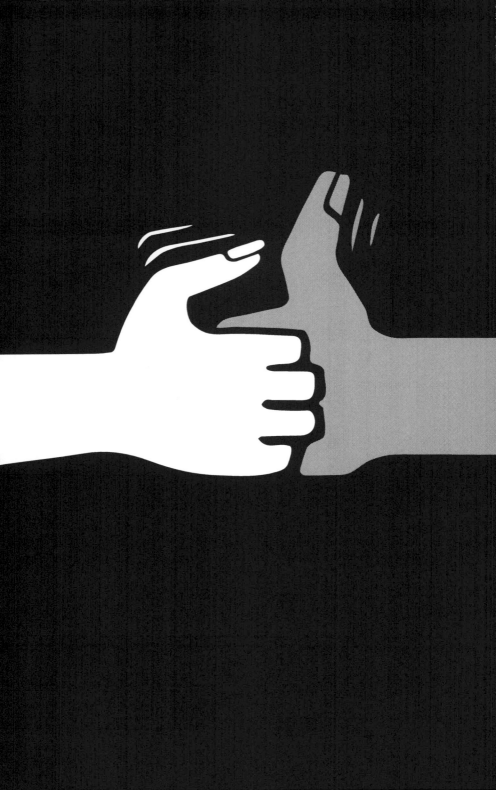

STEP 4

Fight Fair

THE ART OF FIGHTING

Disagreements between you and your Mate are inevitable. Fighting is as intrinsic to a relationship as sex, which happens to be one of the top five issues that couples argue about. The other four are money, work, kids, and housework, but the possibilities are endless.[15]

Happy couples intuitively understand that conflicts are an inevitable part of a relationship, in the same way that nagging physical injuries are an inevitable part of getting older. What matters is not that you fight, it is *how* you fight. You fight to stay together, not to be "right."

Fighting is a cause of divorce only 40 per cent of the time. More often marriages end because, in an effort to avoid disagreements, partners distance themselves so much that their friendship and emotional connection are lost.[16]

Dispute resolution theory suggests "at the earliest possible time and at the lowest possible level, you are expected to recognize and acknowledge conflict and to try to resolve it responsibly."[17]

Let's distill that into three simple elements:

1. Recognize

How do you know you're fighting? You haven't had sex. That's the easy one to recognize. The trickier one to recognize is when your Mate snipes at you in public and then ignores you in private. Don't be fooled; she's fighting with you.

2.   Acknowledge

You have a responsibility to hold up your end. Men's natural tendency is to stick their heads in the sand and wait for the storm to blow over. Sometimes this works, but if this is your default position, you're in trouble. Sooner rather than later, man up and call her on it. Women appreciate a man who brings out their best, not someone who silently acquiesces to their worst.

Let her know you want to talk. "Honey, I've noticed something seems amiss. I'm concerned about it and want to check in."

Notice that you are taking responsibility with "I," not accusing her with "you."

3.   Try to resolve it responsibly

Give your Mate a choice of two windows of time where you have at least 30 minutes free (tonight after dinner? Saturday at brunch?)—not when you're heading out the door or her favorite TV program is about to start.

If she says *now*, that's OK, as long as neither of you is tired/frustrated/angry/hungry. Any of these will sabotage your good intentions, so thank her for being willing to talk, but hold out for a better window of time.

State your complaint succinctly and *stick to one topic*. If you think she's spending too much time with her girlfriends/at the gym and not enough time with you and the kids, that is the topic for today's fair fight.

"Darling, we had dinner together as a family only one night this week. We agreed that we would have dinner at least three times, so we're coming up short. The kids and I miss you. What's up?"

If your Mate turns around and accuses you of watching too much TV/Internet porn/sports and ignoring you, that is tomorrow's fair fight.

"Hmm, I didn't realize that. Maybe you're right. I'm happy to hear what you have to say and talk about it with you, but let's do that next. Right now, let's go back to family dinnertime. You've been missed. How do we get you back, honey?"

But be prepared to cut some slack on this, because the thing you *think* you're fighting about may *not* be the thing your Mate is fighting about. (See *Read the Subtitles*, p. 134). How do you know? Try reality testing the issue. "So honey, if I were to stop watching sports on TV all weekend long, would that make you happy?"

If one of you is losing her/his cool, STOP. Partners often differ in the level of emotional intensity they are comfortable with. Explosive shouting may be how you work through issues, but anger may be your courage to let words fly that will wound your Mate. If your Mate is more rational or prefers an avoidant style, you will come across aggressively. Instead, hit the pause button and tell her, "We need to take a break because we are not fighting fair. Let's pick this up when things are calmer."

Notice the magic "we," not the accusatory "you" or the it's-all-about-me "I." Walk away and give your thinking brain a chance to recover. No one wins an unfair fight.

When you're ready, start on the right foot. "That was over the top. I'm sorry. Can we rewind and try again?"

One final tip is to have a pact. Do not name call or swear at each other. *Ever.* What is acceptable? If you wouldn't say it to your boss or assistant, why would you throw it in the face of the person whom you have sworn to love, honor, and respect above all others? *Hint*: put this in your Declaration of Interdependence.

Contrary to popular superstition, it is OK to go to bed mad. But not two nights in a row.

How do you know the fight is over? You have sex.

How do you know the fight is REALLY over? You feel respected, your Mate feels loved, and you feel closer to each other than you felt before the fight.

THE GRIPE LIST

Sometimes we let things slide. Something is bothering your Mate (or you), but you decide not to say anything and hope it will go away.

Not a chance. It will come back and bite you in the ass.

We've all been there. You do or say some careless thing, which by itself, is no big deal. But it is the proverbial straw that breaks the camel's back of your Mate's ability to tolerate you one second longer. She loses it, and a wave of fury and scorn spews forth, carrying upon it her mental gripe list of all the things that you and the collective universe have done, or not done, since time began.

It's not too late to flip back to *The Art of Fighting* (p. 101). The three elements—recognize, acknowledge, and try to resolve it responsibly—still apply.

Let her blow out her Dragon fire. The only reason you have for waving the white flag of "we'll take this up later" is if name-calling and swearing start up *and* you have a pact banning this. Otherwise shut up and listen the third way (p. 69); her anger needs to dissipate before you have a shot at fighting fair.

THREE MAGIC WORDS:
TELL ME MORE

When we are subjected to something unpleasant, our reflexes kick in and we do one of three things: fight, flight, or surrender. Reflexes are intended to keep us safe from harm and that's a good thing, most of the time anyway.

But there are times when our reflexes get us into trouble. Especially with your Mate. And especially when you're fighting.

Your Mate throws out one of her favorite hooks in the heat of an argument. "That's the third time this week that you said you'd be home for dinner and you weren't. All you care about is work. You don't care about the kids or me."

You feel as though you've been ambushed but your reflex—whichever one kicks in—is only going to get you into more trouble. Unless, of course, she is slinging a frying pan at your head, in which case flight is your best option.

When your Mate is on fire with frustration and anger, you *cannot* put that fire out. If you try to suppress her anger with fight, flight, or surrender, it will end badly.

Fight? Men's favorite verbal fighting tactics are defensiveness and counterattack.

Defensiveness almost *always* escalates a conflict. "I couldn't help it. Something important came up at work."

When you give your "reasons," you are saying to the other person s/he is *without* reason. Telling an angry and upset person that s/he is acting unreasonably is a conflict resolution strategy for the emotionally unintelligent. Maybe your Mate *is* being unreasonable—it happens to the best of us occasionally—but telling her this when she's pissed off is not only ineffective, it's pointing the blame back at her.

Counterattack is even worse. "You should talk. You're the one who spends more time with your mother than with me." Not only are you ignoring your Mate's complaint that you were late for dinner, but you are belittling *her*. Sarcasm and contempt are toxic at the best of times but are especially destructive when they are in response to criticism.

Flight? Whether you give her the silent treatment or flee the room, you are turning away from your Mate. Biologically, men are more easily overwhelmed by conflict than their Mates are, and try to distance themselves from the conflict...and from their Mate.[18] Does this sound familiar? The husband is the stonewaller in 85 per cent of marriages.[19] You may think you're avoiding a fight, but you're avoiding your marriage.

Surrender? "I don't know what you want. Just tell me." If you are in the early days of a relationship, you may be able to get away with playing the clueless card occasionally, but mostly it will backfire. You're telling your Mate that you are clueless about her and about your relationship. Maybe you *are* clueless, but if your default is to abdicate leadership for keeping your relationship together, you're being a wuss.

A wussy male creates the perfect conditions for a woman's inner Dragon to rise up and devour him.

Smart men develop a fourth reflex: *curiosity*. They learn to say, "that's interesting," and invite their Mate to say more, not less. The angrier she is, the more important this is to her. So give her a gift: the opportunity to vent in a way that provides you with *information*, not a withering attack on your manhood.

"That's interesting. Tell me more…"

"That's interesting. Why would you say/ask/do that?"

Don't be a parrot! Watch quality talk show hosts such as Oprah and Ellen and notice how seamlessly they invite—not interrogate—their guests to tell them more. Make it your own.

"I see. Tell me more about that."

"Hmmm, how did that work?"

"Interesting, and then what happened?"

"OK, maybe you're right. What would you like to happen?"

More than 80 per cent of the time, it's the wife who points out the dead fish under the table, while the husband tries to ignore the smell of decay.[20] This happens in *all* relationships, happy and unhappy. By asking your Mate for more information about the state of the dead fish, not only are you giving her the gift of turning toward her, you are giving yourself a gift: *time to think*. You're buying time to switch gears from your fight/flight/surrender reflex to your ass-saving curiosity reflex.

STEP 5

Do the Work:
More Survival Tips

THE
[HOUSEWORK = SEX]
EQUATION

One in two couples fights about housework, according to a survey by the American Cleaning Institute.[21] Typically, a woman's house-cleaning standards are higher than a man's. Before you get righteous, there are exceptions, but, as a general rule, men don't realize how deeply important it is to women to have a clean and orderly nest.

"But I try," you say. "She doesn't appreciate my efforts. It's never good enough." Poor guy, you can't win. Right?

Wrong. When a man does his share (whatever the housework division is between you and your Mate), both he and his wife report a better sex life than in relationships where the wife believes her husband is not doing his share.[22]

There is something about a man who produces shiny, clean, fresh-smelling surfaces that a woman finds irresistible. A sparkling bathroom is a turn-on. A urine-splashed toilet seat—especially one that is left *up*—is revolting.

I have noticed that there are men who love to argue about this, as if there is some logic or rationale that will convince a woman that a befouled toilet is not an impediment to sex. Seriously guys, let me remind you of the blindingly obvious: Do you want to defend pee stains on your toilet seat, or do you want to have more sex?

Not convinced yet? Try letting in this new information:

"The degree of significance attached to not doing a perfect job cleaning the kitchen sink, or putting the cap back on the toothpaste tube, is likely to be in direct proportion to other marital issues of far greater importance."[23] Being constantly resistant to the easy stuff, like throwing your dirty underwear in the laundry hamper, can indicate deeper issues, such as purposeful annoyance, suppressed hostility, and passively-aggressively starting fights.[24] Douches constantly piss off their Mate with the small stuff. Diamonds don't.

A woman's mind is filled with small stuff. And big stuff. Endless lists of things to do. Hire new assistant. Fire under-performing sales rep. Review budget. Pay bills. Buy groceries. Drive kids to sports. Call friend. Walk dog. Book family holiday. Make up guest bedroom before in-laws arrive.

These lists crowd out the "I want sex" part of a woman's brain, blocking her libido like a bad haircut. If the house is clean and tidy, the libido-blocking lists shrink. She can relax, and that is a prerequisite for sex. Cleaning—properly—is an act of service that tells a woman she is respected and supported by a considerate Mate. She is happy, and therefore, you are happy. Happy people have sex more often than unhappy people.

Don't know where to start? You need to learn a woman's C-spots. Tom McNulty describes these as the areas of the house she absolutely, positively needs to be clean.[25] Just as you learn what works and doesn't work in the bedroom, you can learn what works and doesn't work in the bathroom, kitchen, and living room. Try these five easy steps:

1. Make the bed, properly. Repeat *daily*.

2. Do a quick online search of simple housecleaning tips and choose no more than three doable tasks. Keep the list short. As Jason Fried and David Heinemeier Hansson point out in *Rework*, "Long lists are guilt trips...And at a certain point, you just stop looking at it because it makes you feel bad."[26]

3. Grab some cleaning wipes (*hint*: look under the kitchen or bathroom sink), set the timer for 15 minutes, and GO!

When the timer goes off, finish that task, and put the cleaner back where you found it. That's it. You're done.

4. If she notices your efforts and says something, *listen* to her reaction. Let the information in, and don't argue.

If she doesn't notice your efforts, try again, harder.

5. Repeat often.

With a dollop of consideration, this habit can be as automatic (for both of you) as cleaning your teeth. It's only fifteen minutes! You spend more time watching commercials when your favorite TV show is on. A daily cleaning workout can change your relationship forever.

A few notes of caution. One, the secret to housework-equals-foreplay is in *silent* acts of service. Do not point out to her your superhuman cleaning exploits, because boasting is for children. She is turned on by a man who cleans, not a little boy who is showing off.

Two, if you've been a slacker in the cleaning department, she will be suspicious of your motives. Or critical, especially if she has über-high standards. Do not give up. Ask her to show you how she would like it done, and keep tidying and cleaning in 15-minute acts of love. Your persistence will be rewarded.

Three, cleaning the car is *not* housework. The same goes for polishing your golf clubs. Don't argue. They don't count. That's just how it is.

DON'T EXPECT A PARADE

You know how it goes. You notice that your Mate is a bit grumpy—broken sleep, her presentation didn't win the bid, the kids are buzzing on leftover Halloween candy, and the cat threw up on the sofa—and you know it's going to be a tough evening. But you resist the temptation to turn around and head back to the office, and pull out all the stops to make it better for her.

You pour her a glass of wine, order your favorite takeout to be delivered, bathe the kids, and even empty the dishwasher from two days ago.

Your burst of domestic do-gooding fills you with manly pride. You silently acknowledge how far you've come in your relationship with your Mate. You are no longer the center of your universe, the pivotal sun around which the planets revolve. Now you orbit around your Mate and kids, providing for them, caring for them. They are lucky to have you. You rock. You think to yourself, "Surely my Super Guy efforts this evening will be appreciated."

Think again.

Who takes care of dinner, bathes the kids, and empties the dishwasher the other 364 days of the year? Just because you contributed more domestic do-gooding than your Mate tonight, it doesn't entitle you to a parade. There's no round of applause from the kids after bath time. You're not doing her some big favor by taking out the garbage either. Why? *Because you live there too.*

For every hour of your dishwasher-emptying and garbage-taking-out, your full-time working Mate is putting in *more than twice as many* hours of dirty-underwear-picking-up and cat-vomit-removal. "Women do approximately three quarters of household work, a pattern that is evident across all western nations."[27]

It is not just you who is not pulling your domestic weight; it is universally a guy thing, regardless of class, education or income.[28] From 10-year-old boys (who do 35 per cent less housework than 10-year-old girls[29]) to Stanford University male scientists (who do just 28 per cent of the cooking, cleaning, and laundry in their households compared to their female scientist counterparts who do 54 per cent[30]), the gender division of labor inside the household has remained largely unchanged since dinosaurs roamed the earth, despite massive recalibration of the labor outside the home.

Your argument that you work longer hours and earn more income is not relevant to this debate, unless you are one of the lucky ones who has a Mate who stays at home full-time and, if you have kids, they are in school full-time.

You don't "help out" at work, you contribute your share. So don't "help out" at home; contribute your share, just as you do at work. Remember that you are equal partners in your home (just as you are equal partners in your relationship), and equally responsible for its blissful state or otherwise. So when you step up one night and contribute to housework, the world isn't going to tilt on its axis.

Don't be discouraged. Keep up your domestic do-gooding for two nights in a row, then three. Then six out of seven. Keep at it for an entire month.

Now take her in your arms with a smile and ask her if there's anything you can do to help.

EQUALITY

What do these people have in common: the Rolling Stones, Queen Elizabeth II, and Bryan Cranston?

They are in relationships that have *endured*. It may not always be pretty or perfect, but they have stuck it out—together—over the long haul.

Mick Jagger is the flamboyant front man, but the other Stones are equally influential in the Stones' success and staying power and in the band's very *essence*. Prince Philip has played second fiddle for over half a century yet has steadfastly supported his Queen in public while being his own man. Ditto for *Breaking Bad's* Bryan Cranston whose marriage to Robin Dearden has spanned over 20 years. Never mind the Emmys, Bryan brags that he can load a dishwasher like nobody else.[31]

These diverse long-term relationships have one thing in common: the partners have a reasonably equal balance of power. Each person who we think wears the pants knows that the *other* person is the reason that their relationship is great. The person values her/his partner(s) for what s/he brings to the relationship, which makes it better than the sum of the parts.

The couple's value is not measured in paychecks or hours worked but in their commitment to each other. They are quality people who have each other's back.

Assuming your choice of Mate was based on the brain in your head more than the one in your pants, your Mate is a quality person too, a Diamond. You saw her as your equal, possibly even your better, as someone worthy of you and vice versa. So far, so good.

Now for the challenge: how to keep equal over the long haul. At work we are usually rewarded for being right. The more right you are, the more you are promoted, and the more money you earn. One day you become the boss, and the pressure is *really* on to be right.

As a smart boss you would build a great team and listen to it, but you still call the shots. This hierarchy makes sense when your paycheck is a measure, albeit an imperfect measure, of your talent and contribution. But your personal life is not a hierarchy, and there are no paychecks to measure your talent and contribution as a partner to your Mate. In her eyes, you are the guy who didn't put out the garbage.

So regardless of how high you climb in the work hierarchy, do not make the mistake of thinking that you are more important than your Mate. Your impressive job and high rollin' paycheck do not change how much you matter to your Mate in your relationship; they only change the price tag of ending it. The floor still needs sweeping, the garbage still needs taking out, and the toilet still needs your pee wiped off the seat.

If you are engrossed in saving lives or ruling the world to the extent that you can't contribute to household tasks, then hire someone to take your place. Your work commitments do not legitimize your absolution from household tasks any more than your Mate's paid work commitments extend that right to her.

This means that *you* initiate a conversation with your Mate about coming up short on your contribution, and *you* do the work of hiring a cleaner, making sure s/he is doing a great job, and paying her/him.

If your Mate elects to stay at home and raise the kids, take care of aging parents, or manage your household and social life so that you don't have to, get down on your knees and give thanks every day. She has taken on a task that is undervalued and underappreciated but which contributes to families, neighborhoods, and communities in immeasurable ways. I get why 70 per cent of women with children work outside the home, but credit also deserves to go to the 30 per cent of women with children who work *inside* the home. My family has traveled both paths, and neither choice is "better;" you simply do what you need to.

Our society assumes no great skill is involved in taking care of a baby or cleaning a house. People who do get paid for caretaking work (not coincidently, an almost entirely female workforce) are usually paid poorly. Your wonderful Mate has relinquished her status jollies, so despite how important your career is to you and the family balance sheet, don't cluelessly rub her nose in her **un**-career of managing your home and family.

Nothing tests equality in a relationship more than inequality in paychecks. The more your paycheck rises relative to hers, the more risk there is that you will think you get to call the shots. The whiff of superiority will turn to the stench of contempt before you realize it.

Insist on doing your 50 per cent share, and worship your Mate for doing the other 80 per cent of it.

READ THE SUBTITLES

Has your relationship gone from sugar to shit? No matter how much you pretend otherwise, you've lost that lovin' feeling and something is wrong. Whether there is tension, disagreement, or emotionality, you've got conflict. Conflicts are like fish; if you leave them under the table, they will start to smell.

Men have a higher threshold for a smelly fish; they can ignore it a lot longer than most women can. But if you want to survive, you need to take charge of the fish. It is exhausting for women to always be the ones to give the "we need to talk" command while you stick your obtuse head in the sand and wait for it all to blow over.

Show leadership in your relationship by putting the fish on the table and hashing it out before it sours your relationship. But before you can do that, you need to know what the fish *is*.

This is where men get themselves into trouble. They tend to take things at face value, but women are more complicated than that. Sometimes women say what they mean. Often, they do not.

Women say "sure, call me" when they mean "when hell freezes over."

Women say "they're lovely" when they mean "I can't believe you gave me golf clubs for my birthday, you moron."

Women say "are you wearing that shirt?" when they mean "if you wear that, I'm not having sex with you."

Women say "this house is a mess" when they mean "when you and the kids leave your shit all over the place, I feel like your mother-slave. Either clean up after yourself, or hire a cleaner."

Figuring out your fish under the table takes practice. But like anything worth doing, the more you do it, the better you will both become at cleaning out the fish.

Tell her you think something's not right between you. Be your best CEO self—no complaints, criticism, sarcasm, or defensiveness. Turn on your third way of listening and ask her, "Why is that? Tell me more." By the fourth or fifth "why" you should be getting close to the fish.

For example, a common complaint is that one partner—often the guy—works too much. You have a list of reasons why you work long hours, and many of them are valid. Your boss may be demanding, layoffs have piled more work on those still on the payroll, or you need the overtime or billable hours to bolster your paycheck or promotabilty. Or perhaps your job is who you are, and you feel awesome when you're at work, doing your job, and doing it well.

There's nothing wrong with this. On the contrary, your work ethic and commitment may be qualities that attracted your Mate to you in the first place. But if you're consistently putting in so many hours that your Mate feels emotionally disconnected from you, there is a fish under your table.

You: "Sweetheart, something's not right. What's up?" (Starts gently.)

Mate: "You've been working a lot. The kids hardly ever see you. And when you do come home, you're tired and want to be left alone. I feel like I'm doing it all on my own." (Complains with blaming, but expresses her feelings.)

You: "Yeah, I've been working for months on The Big Project and it's been a challenge, especially since we had to let go two of our staff. But I miss you and the kids, and I hate being so tired all the time." (Slightly defensive, but expresses his longing; acknowledges her complaint about his tiredness.)

Mate: "Thanks, we miss you too. What bothers me is that this has happened before. You say you're sorry, and I say it's OK, and we get by for a while. But it's not OK. We need to figure out a better way. I don't want to live like this, waiting for the next big project to take you away again." (Expresses appreciation; goes further into complaint; some sarcasm)

You: "You're right. But when the big projects are underway, I have to work long hours. It's always been that way, you knew that when we got married, and it's not going to change any time soon. But I do miss you and the kids, so maybe we can figure out a way to have more time together in between the big projects." (Affirms; takes responsibility but somewhat defensive; tells her that she and the family matter; expresses willingness to find a solution together.)

Mate: "Yeah, I remember how hard you worked when we first met, but I also remember how much fun we had. And we used to talk more, even when you were working 80 hours a week, so I knew what was going on with you and didn't feel so disconnected. I'd like more of that. Do you have any ideas?" (Acknowledges your contribution; expresses longing; clarifies her need; expresses desire to find a solution together.)

When you uncover the fish, you are looking at the gap between "this person is driving me crazy" and "I love this person." How you deal with that gap will either be your undoing or one of those crazy funny stories you tell your grandchildren when they ask the secret of your long and mostly happy relationship.

APPRECIATION

There are two ways to appreciate your Mate: sincerely and often. When your Mate's happiness is your first waking thought and the last smile at night, it isn't hard to fill the space in between with appreciation. This is one of the most elementary examples of cause and effect: a Mate who is appreciated will reciprocate.

Let's take a moment to make sure we are talking about the same thing. Dictionaries define appreciation as gratitude and thankful recognition of the quality, value, significance, and magnitude of a thing or person. Those four dimensions—quality, value, significance, and magnitude—give marvelous depth to the act of appreciating your Mate.

Tell her she looks gorgeous (quality). Be specific. Tell her she has beautiful eyes, but also praise her body parts that you adore—butt, waist, legs— especially the parts that she is less than happy with. Pay her compliments *outside* the bedroom. Tell her, "You look sexy in that dress," at the in-laws' dinner party or "You're gorgeous; the other women look like peasants beside you," at your annual company picnic. Your sincerity is reinforced when you aren't peeling off her clothes as you steer her toward the bedroom.

Thank her for filling up the kitchen with groceries and putting clean shirts in your closet (value). Ask how her important meeting went and what the highlight of her day was (significance). Tell her that the highlight of your day was coming home to her, knowing you could hold her in your arms and kiss her (magnitude).

Telling your Mate how much you appreciate her is a solid start, but *showing* her your appreciation takes it to another level. Show her how much you appreciate your shared nest by picking up after yourself, and if necessary, picking up after her. Show her how much you appreciate her gorgeousness by ditching your comfy duds and dressing stylishly. After all, a hot woman deserves a stylin' guy on her arm. Show her that you appreciate how hard she works by pouring her a glass of wine and giving her a foot massage *and* your full attention, while she tells you about her important meeting and the highlight of her day.

By all means, go for romantic and extravagant flourishes on special occasions, but a great relationship between two people is built—or destroyed—on the back of everyday life. It's easy to be appreciative when you feel like it, but going the extra mile when you're tired and distracted, or when she's hormonal and cranky, is what separates great relationships from the ordinary.

If you've been a slacker in the appreciation department, you can expect your Mate to be wary or downright suspicious at first. But stay the course and never—*ever*—expect her to have sex with you just because you emptied the dishwasher or gave her a foot rub for the first time since forever.

Your new mantra is show and tell, sincerely and often. A Mate who is on the receiving end of a steady tide of genuine appreciation is one who will make sure her man is on the receiving end of her appreciation.

DEPRECIATION

In the previous chapter, we looked at appreciation in terms of gratitude and thankful recognition. Appreciation has another meaning in the accounting world: the increase in the value of an asset over time. This bland business definition takes on a delightful dimension when applied to relationships. The more you appreciate your Mate—sincerely and often—the more you increase the value of your relationship over time.

This play on the word "appreciation" opens the door to see its opposite: depreciation. Accountants define this as the decrease in the value of an asset over time. In other words, the asset loses economic value through use. For example, a machine wears out over its useful life.

The point is that there is no "steady state" in your relationship with your Mate. Either you are appreciating her and increasing the value of your relationship over time, or you are depreciating her and running down the useful life of your relationship. Great relationships are not self sustaining; they need maintenance, just like your car or your golf swing.

Not appreciating her? Then you're taking her for granted. *Poof!* Your relationship is depreciating right under your nose. Not showing her that she is the center of your universe? Then your relationship is losing ground.

You can either appreciate her sincerely and often, or be prepared to accept the alternatives. At best, you'll have a mediocre marriage. At worst, your relationship will fully depreciate and you'll invest instead in a divorce lawyer.

GO AWAY

Life often gets in the way of living. It also gets in the way of loving. If you want a happier Mate, make time for it.

By making a conscious choice to step away from the busy-ness of your life, you can bring your full attention to your Mate, the goddess. Take charge of *all* the details; do not leave it to your Mate to do anything except block off time from her work. Find a few days where you can both step away without massive inconvenience, put it on the calendar, and make everything else fit around your sacred getaway.

I repeat: it is *your* job to take care of *all* the details. This includes booking the getaway, organizing for the kids and pets to be looked after, asking the neighbors to collect your newspapers and garbage cans, setting the lights on timers—*every*thing.

Goddesses don't do mundane details; they are feted and adored. Arrange to pick her up from work. Be early. Collect her from her desk, flowers in hand and a big adoring grin, as her nosy and deeply impressed colleagues poke their heads out of their cubicles. You've already won major brownie points, but the goddess treatment has only just begun.

Her favorite coffee/water is waiting for her in the cup holder and her favorite music is playing as you whisk her away to a splendid weekend à deux. It doesn't matter whether you drive to a downtown hotel overnight or fly to a luxury resort for a week, the point is you are making your Mate the center of your universe or the way she was when you fell in love with her, before life got in the way. You are celebrating you as a couple, not a birthday or an anniversary, just you-two-together.

During your uninterrupted time together, ask her about you-two-together. What's working? What could be better? What has made her happy lately? What has made her laugh? What does she want more of? Less of? How's the sex? How is your Declaration of Interdependence holding up?

You get the picture. Keep it happy and joyful by celebrating the best of you-two-together and not by amplifying the little things that won't matter in five years' time.

Also, beware of the trap of focusing too much on stuff that came *after* you-two-together. Things like the mortgage or the kids may be important and you can't imagine life without them, but don't be mistaken and think for one minute that they are part of you as a *couple*; you-*two*-together.

If you-two-together are solid, the stuff that came after will be just fine, especially your kids.

(Women are often guilty of putting the kids first. This is to be expected with a new baby, but once s/he can walk, it's time to reclaim the top spot in your Mate's affections. As parents, your job description includes role modeling a healthy and happy relationship, not a child-centered one. If you and the dog are tied for last place in your domestic pecking order, you need to take a stand.)

So go away with your Mate, take the pulse of you-two-together, and celebrate your good fortune in having this great woman by your side.

SEND HER AWAY

Women enjoy the company of other women. They get to talk for hours without someone asking what's for dinner or reaching for the TV remote. Together, women drink too much wine, eat too many nibblies, and wear pajamas all day just because they can.

But all this is an extraneous bonus to the real reason women should spend time away together: women say stuff to other women that they would never say to a man, especially you. This is healthy, and you want to encourage it. Let her share dark secrets with other women, because they will have darker secrets. Your Mate will come back relieved and grateful that she has you and not the morons with whom her friends are sharing their beds.

However, the brownie points you will earn by sending her away and taking care of the house, kids, and Stinky in her absence will evaporate faster than beer at a frat party if she comes home to a mess. *Poof!* When your Mate walks through the front door, you will have the house and children spotless, dinner in the oven, and a glass of wine ready for her. Cue the seven-minute rule. And, of course, you put fresh sheets on the bed, right?

GET REAL

Men are delusional about how much sex they should have. The blame lies not so much with women who won't have sex with them, but with other men who lie about how much sex they are actually having.

Here's the cold, hard truth: the average married or committed guy has sex about once or twice a week, a figure that hasn't changed in more than half a century.[32] A man will have more sex if he's in a new relationship (three to four times) but less sex if he's single (once a week).[33]

The thing about averages is that no one is ever precisely average. If you're working long hours, raising a young family, out of shape, or taking your Mate for granted, your average drops to once a month or even once a year. Statistically, for every one lucky husband having sex every day, there are 40 of you on the once-a-year plan. Most married men think they hit the jackpot if they have sex twice a week.

The bottom line is that sex in a long-term relationship will probably never be "as frequent and delicious as it once was, and if that's what you expect, you are setting yourself and your parter up to fail."[34] As Dr. Helen Fisher of Rutgers University eloquently states, "it is not adaptive to be intensely romantically in love for twenty years...we would all die of sexual exhaustion."[35]

What is reasonable for you and your Mate? Here's your rule of thumb: take the amount of sex you're having with your Mate when your relationship is new, and cut it in half after Year Two. There's *your* best case average.

If you're falling short of this, the two next chapters are for you.

SEX IS NOT NEGOTIABLE

If you've reality-checked your new average, you're falling short and you're not OK with it, rethink your approach. (If your *Mate* is not OK with it, fast forward to the next chapter.) Never—*ever*—present your Mate with your meticulously compiled research and calculator to "prove" that you should be having more sex. To hit your number, work on your approach, not your negotiation skills.

She knows how much sex her friends are having, because women talk about that stuff and—unlike men—they don't exaggerate. Your Mate knows if you're above or below "average"—and she expects *you* to be in charge of doing something about it. Unless you have explicitly agreed that your Mate will initiate lovemaking, it is your responsibility (most of the time) to keep your sex life alive and well.

Does she turn you down? Men complain that when they initiate sex, they overestimate their Mate's desire to get it on. Why? They think their hard-on is a turn-on for their Mate. Not so fast.

Somewhere in the mists of time, the guy forgot about first, second, and third bases. You managed to win over your Mate by hitting *all* the bases when you were courting, right? So why not do your sex life a big favor and take your foot off the gotta-get-laid accelerator. Instead, make sex fun and desirable again.

Try giving her a longer-than-usual kiss just before she heads out the door without you, and enjoy the surprise in her eyes. Arrive at the movies a few minutes early and neck in the back row. Send her love texts during the day. Tell her how hot she looks just as you arrive at her parents' house for dinner. Flirt with her at dinner. Hold your position on first, second, or third base, and let *her* initiate moving forward.

Go back and review *Why Listening Gets You Laid* (p. 66). What is the most common denominator to having more sex? Connecting with your Mate *outside* the bedroom. According to *Men's Health* magazine, "Talking to her—about work, family, the news—is the greatest aphrodisiac for a woman because it establishes a bond of sharing that she equates with romance. To you, it's conversation. To her, it's intimacy."[36]

Here's the paradigm: you feel close to your Mate *after* you've had sex. Your Mate is wired exactly opposite: she needs to feel a bond of intimacy with you *before* she wants sex. No amount of negotiating will change that.

So forget about how much sex everybody else claims to be having and how to negotiate that fallacy for yourself. Turn towards your Mate *outside* the bedroom and save your negotiation skills for the office.

NOT TONIGHT, HONEY

Increasingly, men are saying, "not tonight, honey."[37]

Although sex is one of the Big Five issues that couples fight about throughout their relationship (the other four are money, work, kids, and housework), the conundrum of your Mate having a higher sex drive than you can push your relationship into a new and very stressful zone.

If you're both genuinely happy and satisfied to join the sexless masses, turn the page. If your preferred sex threshold doesn't flatline, read on.

It's always hard to be the one who wants more. "The lower-desire partner has the power to grant or deny—and that often leaves the higher-desire partner feeling powerless and rejected, and the lower-desire partner feeling guilty."[38] And while you are culturally scripted to "expect" to be rejected by women ("it's not me"/"women always turn guys down"), at least your rejection and frustration line up with expectations. If your Mate has the higher desire, however, she doesn't get that reassurance. Neither do you.

Low male libido is more common than you think, but because guys don't say to each other, "Hey, I've been having chubble* lately," men suffer in embarrassed silence.

[*A combination of the word chub (slang for erection) and trouble][39]

While one of my **un**-studies concludes that almost every man known intimately by my female friends hasn't been able to get it up at least once or twice, 40 percent of men over the age of 40 suffer from erectile problems at least occasionally, and the percentage increases with age.[40] The easy erections you had when you were 14 simply aren't going to happen at 40.

If it's so common, why do only a third of chubbled men come forward for help to investigate any underlying medical conditions?[41] Because erectile problems go to the very core of masculinity. Men tie their self-worth into two things—their jobs and their sexuality—which can easily fracture and erode. It can be easier to just stop having sex with your Mate and sleepwalk through your relationship than risk embarrassment.

Any number of psychological or physical factors could put your libido in a tailspin, and often the isues combine. Stress, lack of sleep, obesity, fatigue, overall poor health, excessive masturbation (usually attended by a virtual private harem of gorgeous smiling hotties who never criticize or reject), alcohol problems, hormone imbalances (notably low testosterone), depression, and some antidepressants all interfere with sex. If you and your Mate have a less-than-great relationship with problems such as lack of trust, financial issues, or pressure from kids, sex takes a double whammy. It becomes a cycle; one problem exacerbates another, and before you know it, neither of you can remember what came first.

When sex evaporates from a relationship, men and women agree on one thing: that the other person is responsible.[42] Guys mostly say their partners are depressed and angry; they, on the other hand, are adventurous and enjoy sex. Women say the same thing. Somehow we would all be having adventurous and passionate sex if it weren't for the unadventurous, depressed, and angry Mate lying on the other side of the conjugal bed.

It's imperative to have two frank conversations: 1) talk with your medical professional to check for any possible physical conditions; 2) turn to your Mate to examine what's going on in your relationship.

If you've been abstaining from sex, you've probably been abstaining from conversation too. Take a deep breath, and tell her, "Honey, this is really embarrassing, but things aren't working for me in the bedroom. Something's not right, and I think we need some help."

Talking about sex can be tricky for any couple, but there is simply no other way. Withholding sex and still demanding that your Mate be monogamous is selfish and, for many couples, a Deal Breaker.

Your choices are to either to either approach the issue with maturity and compassion, or to suffer in silence while your relationship disintegrates.

A guy who is willing to ask for help from his Mate—and his doctor—is taking a big, difficult step to try to solve the problem. Miracles can happen when a woman is motivated to help her guy cope with his erratic or nonexistent enthusiasm between the sheets.

THE FEELINGS DEBATE

Men have come a long way, baby, but their ability to deal with a woman's feelings invariably has room for improvement.

The most common mistake men make is to ignore, or worse, dismiss a woman's feelings. Men try to take control of *their* feelings and don't expect anyone to be responsible for them. If only women would control their feelings and not be so *emotional*, everyone could live happily ever after, right?

Wrong. Deploying logic all the time makes you about as attractive as Mr. Spock in *Star Trek*. His sex life is widely debated in certain circles on the Internet, but once every seven years seems to be the consensus. If that falls short of your expectations, leave your logic at the office and pay attention. Your survival pathway lies directly behind the obstacle we will call Her Feelings.

Feelings simply *are*. They lie on a feelings spectrum that ranges from *whatever* to *every effing thing sends me off the deep end*. Where you and your Mate are positioned on that spectrum depends on three things: (i) the cards your parents' genes dealt you; (ii) how evolved you are in recognizing and handling your feelings; and (iii) the crap that you are currently dealing with.

It is easy to be calm and reasonable when that trifecta is aligned, but if everything that matters to you—family, work, finances, health—is going pear shaped at the same time, you can expect volatility even when the trigger is not significant in the grand scheme of life.

Regardless if life is rosy or turning to shit, here is what I know to be true: our feelings are perhaps the only thing that we cannot be wrong about. If you *feel* pain, you're not mistaken in that *feeling*. Perhaps the *source* of the pain is mistaken, such as the phantom limb pain that amputees experience, but the *experience of feeling pain* is genuine.

Saying something careless or forgetting your anniversary may cause your Mate to experience pain. Her feelings have been genuinely hurt as much as if you literally punched her in the heart—and *you* are the source of it. Not her past boyfriends, not her period, not her overbearing boss—*you*. Sure, she may be overreacting (see above), but that does not make her pain any less in this particular moment.

Denying Her Feelings will only make things worse and cause her to decide *never, ever, ever* to have sex with you again, because you are a cruel and heartless Douche. Which you are *not*, of course. So do yourself a favor and learn the language of acknowledging Her Feelings (and your own). You want neither to fear nor ignore Her Feelings. Rather, you want to bring them out into the open, because her unacknowledged feelings are an obstacle.

You don't need to take responsibility for Her Feelings, but you do need to pay attention to whatever is causing her to be upset/frustrated/mad as hell.

To get Her Feelings in the open, help her out.

"You seem really angry; tell me what's going on."
Or,

"You sound upset; did I do something to bother
you?"

Instead of saying, "I don't know why you're so
upset that I forgot our anniversary," try:

"I can see you're upset because I forgot our
anniversary. I'm sorry. I didn't mean to hurt you. It's
not a big deal to me. Tell me why it's important to
you."

In one simple statement, you've brought Her
Feelings out into the open. By naming Her Feelings,
you've acknowledged them.

And for the top-of-the-class award, you might
round out your new approach to Her Feelings by
adopting the mantra of one of our wisest, most
happily married friends: " I'm sorry; I was wrong."

MAKE ROOM

When you find someone you care about, you make room for her in your life. The opposite is also true: if you don't care enough about someone, you don't make room for her. It's that simple.

Long-term partners say the best way to improve their relationship would be to spend more time together. In the same way that you made room in your life to date when you were single, you need to make room to date your Mate. It can be as simple as locking eyes with your Mate and asking, "How was your day, beautiful?" or something more choreographed such as whisking her away for a weekend à deux.

I can hear some of you thinking, "But I have a busy life! After working all day, going to the gym, spending time with the kids, walking the dog, cleaning the car/yard/house, and playing golf with the guys, there's not much time left in a week. I'm usually tired, and she's *always* tired. In fact, she hardly even notices me."

Breaking news: work, kids, commuting, TV, Internet, fitness, chores, and hobbies suck up your best hours. The average couple spend just *four minutes a day* together. Your Mate is getting leftovers, the crumbs from your table of life. How important do you think that makes her feel? It may help explain why you may be getting the crumbs or leftovers from her life.

"But she knows I love her. I told her when we got married." Unless you got married this morning, your Mate is probably overdue to hear those words. But even if you tell your Mate that you love her, how are you *showing* her that you love her?

Make room for your Mate by putting her at the top of your list. Set a reminder in your calendar to send her a thinking-of-you text or to pick up her favorite wine/sushi/chocolate on the way home. If your Mate's happiness is a daily recurrence on your radar, *your* happiness will blip on her radar too.

STEP 6

Own Your Shit

STOP WITH THE EXCUSES

Defensiveness is a natural reflex. We react to complaints and criticism by defending our innocence or explaining circumstances beyond our control. "I can't believe you're mad because I'm half an hour late. My meeting ran over time and I got caught in traffic."

You probably don't even realize you're being defensive. Often it is such an integral part of our behavior with others that it's part of our personality. Here are different forms that defensiveness can take:

Justification

"I have to work long hours; everyone in the office does."

"I have to be there; people depend on me."

"I tried but ran out of time."

Counterattack

"I would pick up my dirty clothes if you didn't dump your purse and coat and stuff on the kitchen counter when you walk in the door."

"I would help with the housework if you helped with the yard work/to bring home (more) bacon."

"I spend less time at the golf course than you spend with your mother."

"Why can't you be more supportive?"

Blame

"It wasn't my fault I was late; the traffic was bad."

"You are so hard to please. If I'm a minute late, you're all over my ass."

"You don't understand how much pressure I'm under at work."

"If you loved me, you wouldn't be mad all the time."

"I wouldn't have to look at other women if you would have (more) sex with me."

Manipulation

"I have to work weekends if we want to get ahead."

"If you looked like her, I wouldn't spend all my time at the office or on the golf course."

"If you loved me, you would have sex with me."

If your Mate calls you on your shit, do not make excuses. Your excuses are no grounds for forgiveness. Rather, they will work against you: defensiveness is like blood in the water to a shark.

She likes to go to bed by 10:00 p.m. because she is an early riser. You prefer to stay up late when the house is quiet and work. She wants you to come to bed.

Mate: "You're always up late and working. Why can't you come to bed with me once in a while?"

You: "You're right. I've been spending a lot of time on the new project, and I'm going to be busy with it for another few weeks."

Mate: "But do you have to work late *every* night?"

You: "Um, yes, probably. But let's find some middle ground. How about you run a bath and climb in. I'll finish up here in a few minutes and join you. In the morning I'll skip the gym and go into the office extra early instead."

When you stop with the excuses and your defensiveness takes a hike, you make room for openness instead of resistance, resolution instead of conflict, and more sex instead of her chilly back in bed.

APOLOGIZE RIGHT

"I'm sorry; I was wrong."

All you need to know is contained in that line. If this is already your mantra with your Mate, collect $200, pass go, and give this book to someone who needs it more.

However, because saying those words is so far outside some men's comfort zones, here is the rationale for why they should be *your* mantra.

Everybody screws up, big time and small time. Maybe you spent Saturday afternoon detailing your car when you were supposed to be cleaning the yard for the annual Cinco de Mayo fiesta that your Mate insists upon. Maybe you talked to the cute new intern in the sexy dress at the Christmas party. Or maybe you had an affair with her.

You have been a Douche; that is an inviolable fact in her mind. What is not yet certain is precisely *where* your culpability lies on your Mate's you're-a-Douche scale. Was it an innocent mistake, a thoughtless word that triggered bad memories? Or a what-was-I-thinking colossal blunder that violated her strongest values? This is for *her* to determine, not you.

Regardless of where you sit on her you're-a-Douche scale, your Mate is angry. Resentful. Deeply wounded. And she is under no obligation to forgive you.

If you have built a great relationship with her, she is more likely to cut you some slack and believe that you are sincere when you say you're sorry. However, the more you try to excuse your Douche behavior, the more you throw fuel on your funeral pyre.

And saying "I'm sorry; I didn't mean it that way" or "I'm sorry if you feel that way" is worse than not bothering to apologize in the first place. You are faking an apology by pretending you're sorry then converting it into an insult. You're only sorry that your Mate was too *emotional* or *inept* as to misunderstand you. What are you, a politician? Your sorry/not sorry doesn't fool anyone except yourself. And your Mate is absolutely not going to respect a man who isn't man enough to apologize right.

So smarten up and own your shit, even if you think your Mate's you're-a-Douche scale is way off. A speedy and sincere apology—"I'm sorry; I was wrong"—shows her that you're a class act who accepts responsibility.

Still not convinced? Imagine that your Mate borrowed your favorite T-shirt from your college sports glory days. Someone with coffee bumped into her, and now there's damage. "Not my fault," she says. "Some idiot did a hit-and-run and spilled coffee all over me. I don't know why you're mad. I didn't mean it, and it's just an old smelly T-shirt. I'll buy you a new one."

How sincere does her apology sound to you? Does she genuinely understand what the T-shirt represented to you? Your zenith as a college athlete, the glory days of your youth, prowess, and potential? Man, you were unstoppable. And now it has double-shot, no-whip mocha latte stains all over the front, and she just doesn't get it.

How different would your reaction be if she said with speed and sincerity, "I'm sorry. I was wrong." Now *that* is apologizing right. Your T-shirt would still be ruined, but *you* know that *she* knows that she has been a Dragon and atonement is in order.

STEP 7

Take a Stand

OTIS GOT IT RIGHT

On an unseasonably warm Valentine's Day in New York City in 1967, a young African-American woman sat at the piano and recorded an incendiary song that changed her career. Aretha Franklin would become the Queen of Soul, and *R-e-s-p-e-c-t* would become the battle cry for women's rights (and the civil rights movement).

Ironically, the song was written by a man. Two years earlier Otis Redding had written and recorded *Respect*. It was one of his favorite songs—a man's plea for respect and recognition from a woman when he comes home.

Since then the word *respect* has been horribly misused and abused. Seniors lament its disappearance, long-term couples lose it, Gen X demands it, tweens can't spell it, let alone show it, and even toddlers can act as if the world owes them a favor.

What *is* respect? According to the *Macmillan* dictionary, it is defined as "a feeling of admiration that you have for someone because of their personal qualities, their achievements, or their status, and that you *show* by treating them in a polite and kind way" (emphasis added).

What is interesting is what it is *not*. Respect is not *saying* the word; it is the *showing* that counts. Respect is a behavior, not a word.

This is how you might show respect at the end of a long day when you're both tired, and your Mate is nowhere in sight and has dropped the ball with dinner.

You: (ring, ring) "Hi gorgeous, I just got home and I guess you're still at work. I know it's your turn to cook dinner. But it's late, you're probably tired, and so am I, so I took a pizza out of the freezer for dinner. It'll be ready in 20 minutes. OK with you?"

Her: "Sorry! I didn't realize the time! Sweetie, thanks for sorting out the pizza. I'm leaving now and will be there in 15 minutes. I'll pick up a salad on the way. And I'll cook you something special on Friday night. OK with you?"

You: "That sounds wonderful. Can't wait to see you. Drive safely. I love you."

The *absence* of respect is being inconsiderate.

You: "Hey, I've just walked in the door. It's late, I'm tired and hungry, and there's no sign of you or dinner. You know whose turn it is, right? So, when is dinner going to be on the table?"

The *opposite* of respect is contempt, which is one of Dr. Gottman's four predictors of divorce. (p. 181)

You: "I've just walked in the door. It's late, I'm tired, and hungry, and there's no effing dinner. Is it too much to ask that you make dinner when it's your turn? You're doing this a lot. I'm ordering myself a pizza; just as well I have them on speed dial."

Click.

Respect is not just *what* you say; it's *how* you say it. Tone is a killer. If your Mate is being disrespectful, take control. Call her on it immediately. Let's flip this around and assume it's *your* turn to cook dinner, you're stuck at the office, and she has just chewed you out.

You: "I'm sorry. I didn't realize the time! You must be starving, you poor thing. But, honey, that doesn't mean you have to be rude. Would you speak to your [boss/assistant/customers] the way you just spoke to me?"

If she doesn't back off, disengage until she reclaims her manners.

"Sweetie, I screwed up with dinner and I'm sorry, but you need to own your behavior. Let's give this some space; we can take it up later."

Then end the call, calmly.

When you think the time is right, restart the conversation.

You: "I'm sorry about dropping the ball on dinner tonight, and I will make sure that doesn't happen again. But it doesn't give you—or me—permission to be rude/disrespectful or to start swearing/name-calling/throwing teapots. Can we rewind and try this again?"

Respect is foundational to any worthwhile relationship, especially one with your Mate. Write it into your Declaration of Interdependence. Insist on it. So that even when it gets ugly and you don't like each other very much, you can trust each other to show a little r-e-s-p-e-c-t when you come home. Hey baby.

LUMBERJACKS AND WOODPILES

Women are crazy. They find a wonderful man, fall in love with him, warts and all, and then they set about their life's work of fixing him. She is a lumberjack, and he is a woodpile. Just a bit more whittling away at him and he'll be perfect.

Men are clueless. They find a wonderful woman who falls in love with them, warts and all, and then they become complacent. They become an older, balder, droopier version of their twenty-something-year-old selves. Forty-something is the old twenty-something: same buddies, same jokes, same moves on the dance floor—and in the bedroom.

Take a good look in the mirror. So you see a long-past-expiry-date version of your high school grad photo, or do you see a man who is trying to be the best version of himself? A man who consciously keeps upgrading himself, in the same way that he upgrades his phone, laptop, or TV. A man who is diligent about being a great partner for his appreciative Mate?

If you can truthfully answer "yes" to being the best version of yourself, then you can truthfully take a stand against your lumberjack Mate. Let her know that she needs to put down her axe and appreciate the great Mate that you are trying your best to be.

Sam was complaining about his Mate, Julie, to whom he had been married almost 20 years. Sam had worn cowboy boots since his college days. He was comfortable in his boots and wore them *everywhere*—barbeques, parent-teacher meetings, weddings, funerals. Julie felt it was time for a change. Couldn't Sam wear something dressier when they went somewhere nice? So Julie bought Sam an expensive pair of classy dress shoes, which he refused to wear and took them back to the store for a refund.

Sam complained to anyone who would listen that Julie was crazy. Sam had worn cowboy boots since forever; they were part of his identity, and he would not let Julie change him. What was good enough for Julie 20 years ago was good enough today.

Sometimes it takes great restraint to refrain from smacking people on the side of the head and asking them if they are for real. If Sam had simply asked the question, "Hey beautiful, I love my cowboy boots and I thought you loved them too. What changed?" they might have avoided divorce.

It wasn't the cowboy boots that pissed off Julie; it was the complacency. Sam was stuck in a time warp—same buddies, same jokes, same cowboy boots—and same moves in the bedroom. Sam was a decent man—faithful, employed, and good natured—but he was as stale as grandma's Christmas fruitcake in July. Julie wasn't a lumberjack with an axe; she was a lively, vibrant, and fun woman who was stuck with a man who had been awesome 20 years ago but who had allowed himself to get stuck in a rut and go stale.

Dana and Jack were the flip side of this same coin. Dana and Jack decided to buy furniture for a new home they had just bought together. Dana was excited by the prospect of spending weekends wandering furniture stores hand in hand with her man, making their dream house come to life.

But after one weekend of hand-holding and wandering, Jack checked out. Jack gave Dana carte blanche to buy whatever she wanted that fit their wish list and budget, and he headed for the golf course with his buddies.

Dana was upset but also puzzled. Why didn't Jack want to spend weekends with her looking at furniture? Jack had played every Saturday with these guys for years. Surely he could skip a few games. How could golf be more important than making their new home perfect? How could Dana's happiness not matter?

Dana was crazy. She chose to ignore two important facts: One, most straight men have zero interest in furniture shopping. A man's sofa needs are simple and easily met. Is the sofa comfy? Check. Can you see the TV properly? Check. Is it in the budget? Check. If she wants to spend weeks or months looking at identical—to him—sofas, then that's fine for her, but a man has other ways he would rather spend his free time.

The other, more important, fact is that Jack had been playing golf on Saturday with his buddies long before she came into the picture. Dana knew about Jack's Saturday golf habit but assumed that *he would change*. A bit of axe-whittling to chip away the golf flaw, and Jack would be perfect. Did they ever have a meaningful conversation about Jack's Saturday golf? About other things that were important to them? Nope.

Jack needed to take a stand and tell Dana to put down her axe. Jack deserved her respect for his longstanding Saturday golf commitment, and Dana deserved the courtesy of a conversation—initiated by Jack—about golf and about *flexibility*. In order to make room for Dana, perhaps Jack would be willing to forego golf one Saturday each month to spend it with her, gracefully doing whatever she wanted. Perhaps if or when kids came along, Jack would cut back golf to every second week. Or perhaps Jack absolutely would never give up Saturday golf while he still had a pulse. Whatever. This type of conversation only becomes difficult *when you don't have the conversation.*

DON'T FEED THE DRAGON

Even the most reasonable person will behave unreasonably from time to time. Your Mate is no exception. Whether she is PMS-ing or her world is imploding on all fronts at once, the day will come when your Mate causes you to shake your head in disbelief as she demonstrates that women are crazy.

A wise man knows when to let the small stuff go by but not the *big* stuff. Paralysis and/or flight are not options that will sustain a great relationship. Only martyrs and fools act like stone walls, saying nothing as they hide behind the TV remote, at the office, or on the golf course in the hope that their Mate will take herself back across the Dragon line under her own recognizance. Maybe you can get away with this in the early days of your relationship, but you are setting a precedent that will backfire. Get your practice in while the honeymoon lasts.

If unchecked, wherever your Mate's outburst stops today will become the *starting point* of her outburst next time. Her Dragon behavior will escalate—and it is *your* response that either feeds her Dragon or helps the Dragon fire to die down gracefully. The longer you ignore it, the higher the stakes.

A couple had been married for 25 years. They were a great team, well matched in smarts, interests, and goals, with three awesome kids. Marly was creative, fearless, and gregarious, an ideal Mate for Ivan as his career took off. As Ivan bounded up the corporate ladder, they traveled and entertained important people around the world.

But over time their witty banter shifted; Marly's funny-*ha-ha* stories about Ivan became funny-*mean*. Ivan was skillful in changing the subject and distracting their guests—and Marly—from her diatribe. But Ivan never called Marly on it, and her inner Dragon remained unchecked. Marly's funny-mean banter escalated until there wasn't much that was funny; it was mostly plain mean. Eventually Ivan sat there with a hangdog face and suffered her jabs in silence, like a martyr. Until he quietly announced to Marly that he was filing for divorce, and he left. Family and friends were sad, naturally, but not particularly surprised. Ivan had taken a stand, but it was 20 years too late.

When your Mate crosses the line from temporary insanity to Dragon, take a stand and call her on it. "Hey gorgeous, I notice that you've been yelling at the computer/slamming doors and/or saying things about me/my buddies/my mother that I don't like. It's OK to be mad/upset, but it's not OK to take it out that way. Can you tell me what's bothering you?"

Then the smart guy (that's you) listens carefully, not to defend himself or to seize ammunition for a counterattack (which, incidentally, only provides more fuel for her Dragon fire), but for *new information*.

What is *really* upsetting her? Did her important meeting go badly? Did your mother make a sweet-coated snide remark? Does she resent getting the leftovers from your life while you work insane hours because you love to? (Translation: she misses you!) Or is she simply off her game and wound up but not sure why?

Keep listening, ready to ask the ass-saving question, "What can I do to help?" But also be ready to rein her in if she crosses the Dragon line again.

"Hey beautiful, thanks for telling me. I want to know more and I want to help, but I'm asking you to tell me without attacking and swearing. You wouldn't do that with your boss or coworkers, so it's not OK to do that with me, the love of your life who worships the ground you walk on." (Cue your best goofy smile.)

Taking a stand—early on, respectfully—is integral to a great relationship. *You* get to set the gold standard for having difficult conversations together. Regardless of the smoke and flames that may erupt initially, your Mate will respect you for showing leadership and for caring. By all means, call a time-out if your eyebrows are singed. But if you handle it properly, taking a stand will build trust and intimacy with your Mate.

WHEN SHE *IS* WRONG

We all get it wrong sometimes. That includes you. And—gasp—even your gorgeous Mate. What matters is not so much that she is wrong, but how big a deal it is to *you*.

Is it small potatoes or a big deal? No couple has the same scale: what causes a huge rift for one couple may leave another couple shrugging their shoulders and wondering whatever.

The small stuff is mildly irritating, even amusing, such as when your Mate scores her third parking ticket that month in *your* car, or when she calls your boss "Dan" when he insists on "Daniel." You may choose to let the small stuff slide. For your sanity, I recommend this approach. In fact, this capacity to overlook small stuff is a talent that long-term happy couples share.[43]

The let-the-small-stuff-slide approach works as long as you don't resurrect the wrongs as evidence against your Mate later on. If you let something slide, then consider it gone forever.

If you're not sure, check your Declaration of Interdependence. If her wrong-ness violates any of your DOI principles, then odds are you need to man up and call her on this. Burying your head in the sand may work for you in the short term because you avoid incurring her wrath. But in the long run, you're acting like a wuss and feeding her Dragon. She deserves to know, because you care.

Calling her on her wrong-ness—and, by inference, your right-ness—isn't easy. But how *you* handle the conversation will influence how mad she gets and how long you are frozen out of the bedroom.

Give her the news. Lay all your cards on the table. You're not playing poker. If you hold back some information and play your cards selectively to gain an advantage, you are playing *her*. She will despise you for undermining your relationship, and she may feel entitled to manipulate you in return.

There needs to be trust for your Mate to open up, to be vulnerable. Only by opening up to you in trust can she allow in the new information you are giving her; in other words, that something she did or said was big-time wrong. So give her the news, all of it, and then listen the third way. (p. 69)

You: "Honey, something has been bothering me and I want to talk to you about it. Is now a good time?"

Her: "Um, yeah?"

You: "OK, thanks. Yesterday was my birthday and nothing happened. No card, no gift, no cake, nothing special for dinner, no nothing from you. What happened yesterday?" (Starting nicely with a complaint, not criticism; seeking new information.)

Her: "Oh, I forgot. It's been so busy lately. It's no big deal." (Excuse; stone wall)

You: "It's a big deal to me. Is anything wrong?" (Statement; seeking new information again)

Her: "Sweetie, I didn't want to worry you, but there are rumors about layoffs at work. I'm worried sick and can't think of anything else. I can't believe I missed your birthday. I'm sorry."

You: "Thanks, I appreciate that. No wonder you're distracted. Let's go out for dinner tonight and you can tell me more about what's going on at work."

BE READY FOR THE FALLOUT

You have done your best. In your most objective, caring, articulate way, you have given your Mate the news that she was wrong. Now you need to zip it and give her the floor. You don't know where your Mate will go with this. In all likelihood, neither does she.

Stay with her; by giving your Mate the opportunity to vent—even if sarcasm and criticism rear their ugly heads—she will calm down eventually. If you try to stifle her ("you're exaggerating", "calm down"), she may get a dose of what one of my friends calls mad cow disease, and it's not pretty.

Your Mate may be devastated, angry or defensive, or all three, and more. You-screwed-up conversations are like going out in the rain: you are probably going to get wet, so have your umbrella ready.

For the academically inclined and research junkies, here's some dispute resolution theory for you to ponder. It makes for an excellent umbrella.

In any dispute, there are three elements or layers. Much like the three sides of a triangle, if any one of the elements is not repaired, the dispute collapses on itself in a messy heap.

The three elements of your dispute are:
1. The *things* you are negotiating about, e.g., money or housework (substantive interests)

2. A *fair opportunity* to put forward your points of view, or the feeling that you have been heard (procedural interests)
3. The feeling of *acceptance that your viewpoint is valid* (psychological interests)

It is Door #3 that men stumble over. You can negotiate the fairest outcome in history—a win-win that would get you a stellar bonus and promotion in the business world—but if you think her viewpoint is silly or her feelings are wrong, your dispute is *not* resolved. Men wonder why women keep coming back to a particular issue long after it was a done deal. It's because her viewpoint was pooh-poohed.

When you dismiss your Mate's viewpoint as silly or wrong, it tends to slink away, hide under a rock, grow ten times as big, and come back to bite you in the ass. Your survival lies in accepting that you will *never* be right in arguing that her viewpoint is wrong. Your Mate's viewpoint is valid to *her*. It is no less valid to *her* than your viewpoint is to *you*.

If it helps to get your head around this female logic, know that accepting that her viewpoint is valid does not mean that you have to agree with it. Just because your Mate believes something to be true does not make it so. (Ditto for your beliefs.)

Instead of banging your logical left brain on Door #3, try taking the dispute gracefully through it. "Gorgeous, I hear what you're saying, and I accept that your viewpoint is important to you. But I have a different point of view, and that's important to me. Knowing that, can we put our clever heads together and try to find a solution that we can both be happy with?"

THE BOTTOM LINE

You have tried, *really* tried, to make your relationship work, but the Dragon is impervious. Your Mate is making your life miserable, and the thought of spending the rest of your life with her fills you with despair.

She deserves to know. Tell her.

1.   Tell her where you are at.

"Darling, I love you. But I don't like *us*. Together. You're unhappy and so am I. Desperately so. If I thought the rest of our lives were going to be like this, I couldn't do it."

2.   Tell her what you want.

"I don't want to be with anyone else; I want to be with *you*. But like we used to be, not like this."

3.   Tell her the consequences.

"If we can't turn us around, we are headed for divorce."

Play this card judiciously. It should be the only one left in your hand, the final desperate measure that may pull your relationship back from the brink of divorce.

This plea from the heart may rescue your relationship from the scrap heap. Give it a shot; you've got nothing to lose.

WHAT ARE THE SIGNS?

One in two marriages ends in divorce within seven years. Which flip of the coin are you on? Dr. John Gottman has developed a scientific basis for predictors of divorce, and can predict 91 times out of 100 who will be divorced four years later.[44]

The single most potent contributor to divorce is—wait for it—the *husband's* disappointment with the marriage. In the studies, marriages where the husband was "low in fondness, low in we-ness, low in expansiveness, while also being high in negativity and marital disappointment" ended in divorce.[45] *Your* behavior—not your Mate's—is the best barometer of the health of your marriage.

But what about couples who fight? Aren't they the ones in trouble? Not at all. The study found that being angry with each other was as characteristic of stable, happy couples as it was of unstable or unhappy couples.[46] Frequent arguing does not mean you're headed for divorce. It's about fighting fair—arguing for what's fair, and communicating more passionately so your Mate understands how strongly you feel about a particular issue—*and* repairing the relationship afterward. Stable and happy couples can have difficult and painful fights where they have miscommunication and hurt one another's feelings, but they work through these hurts to de-escalate the negativity and anger, and to restore their bond.

In contrast, unhealthy couples fight *un*fairly. They pull out their weapons and ammunition—criticism, defensiveness, contempt, and stonewalling—and open fire. Gottman calls these the Four Horsemen of the Apocalypse.[47] These bad boys sneak up on unhealthy couples and take them down. The unhappy wife and her disappointed husband involve themselves in each other's mistakes. They focus on imperfections and what is missing, rather than on what is there and working.

Women favor criticism. "I asked you to pick up three things on the way home and the only thing you bothered to remember was the beer. I can't rely on you to do anything right."

Men favor stonewalling. "You are so hard to please. So what if I forgot your lemons and...ah, that other thing...whatever it was. It's not the end of the world."

He switches on his screen of choice and tunes out. She fumes, slamming drawers and pans in the kitchen as she prepares dinner, or she calls her best friend and gives an angry summary of her Mate's shortfalls since the day they met. They have withdrawn from each other and left the door open, not for reconciliation, but for the Four Horsemen to ride on in. The ending point of one confrontation becomes the starting point for the next one.

Emotional disengagement and withdrawal is contagious; your stonewalling eventually becomes mutual. The relationship collapses in the absence of the vital signs of happy and healthy couples: affection, shared humor, question-asking, and active interest.

Don't confuse a good partner with a bad relationship. Couples can be shocked when they become unhappy with each other. You realize that you have fallen out of love before you truly develop love for each other. Check your vital signs carefully before you decide to head for the exit.

THE LIGHTNING ROD

Not all of us radiate sunshine and light every waking hour. Sometimes we are simply off our game, and other times our day goes downhill from the moment we realize that we slept through the alarm. We feel like the fire hydrant at a dog show. And so we push back against the barrage of bad and ugly that life is throwing at us and spread the foulness by projecting our angst onto anyone with a pulse.

There are some people whose sole response is the latter. They have only one gear: it wasn't their fault; someone else was to blame. You've heard their stories, about the bad driver who took up two parking spaces and "made her" scratch the car as she squeezed into a too-small parking space...to the useless co-worker who left the photocopier without paper and made him late for a meeting, because he had to figure out where the paper supplies were stashed and then he had to fill up the stupid machine. These folk would be just fine, thank you, if they weren't surrounded by idiots.

These folks are the Blamers. And if your Mate is a card-carrying member of the League of Blamers, those idiots who surround her include you.

Nothing you do is right or good enough. You've read this book, diligently tried the seven-minute rule, minded your manners, appreciated her, fought fair, got real, dodged minefields, stopped criticizing, read the subtitles, took a stand, and gave her the bottom line. But to no avail. Your Mate keeps the world—and especially you—in the crosshairs for target practice.

Perhaps it's not *you*, it's *her*.

Have you considered that your Mate may be locked in a power struggle with you? Your relationship is the canvas on which she is painting her insecurities and dreams about life. She holds you entirely responsible for fulfilling every one of her needs, desires, and goals.

You are the lightning rod for her disappointment—with herself. She blames you, tries to control you, and demands that you change. *Yesterday.* And no matter how much you change and try to make her happy, you fall short.

Your Mate is a Dragon to her unhappy, fire-breathing core that even the World's Greatest Guy And Best Partner Ever couldn't appease. It's time for the $60,000 question: how's that working for you?

STAY OR GO

You chose the wrong Mate, your relationship is on life support despite your heroic efforts to revive it, and your life is a living hell. So what are you going to do about it?

You have two choices: stay or go.

Staying is not the same as doing nothing. Doing nothing is for wusses. Doing nothing is an open invitation for Gottman's Four Horsemen of the Apocalypse—criticism, defensiveness, contempt, and stonewalling—to fester and poison you both. Any sympathy that your family and friends have for your sorry situation will dwindle; they will avoid your unhappy company and mutter behind your back about wanting to kick your sorry ass for being so lame. Doing nothing is not an option; it's a one-way ticket to misery.

Staying is tough. You shut and bolt the exit doors because you truly believe that you and your Mate are together, no matter what, until death do us part. However there is hope: studies of 700 ready-to-split couples found that two-thirds of them who stayed married were happy five years later.[48] Through sheer tenacity, they turned down the frequency and volume of the Four Horsemen, adjusted their expectations, and realized that a good partner had been by their side all the time; it was their relationship—how they related to each other—that sucked.

If you stay, start by fixing your side. Smarten up your appearance, get some exercise, and do something—*anything*—different. Like emptying the dishwasher, taking up a new hobby you always wanted to try, or doing that new hobby with your daughter. You'll feel happier, more connected, and more *interesting*. Feeling good about yourself is addictive and contagious. Maybe your Mate will catch it too.

THE EXIT

You thought you found your Mate for life. You pinky swear that you have given her your best, and there's *nothing* left. You score 10 out of 10 for trying to make it work.

What if you *truly* have given it your all and your relationship still sucks? At least one of you is desperately unhappy, and you're all out of ideas. Your horse is dead; it's time to get off: you have bet your life on the wrong Mate.

It is time to head for The Exit, but *how*? Breaking up is hard to do, but staying because you're too chicken to call it quits is worse.

Practice. Write down what you need to say to your Mate and read it aloud to yourself. Keep it short; it's not a lecture. It's not a conversation either; you've had plenty of those already, and they didn't resolve anything, right? If you think you need to have another conversation with your Mate, you're not ready for The Exit.

Forget trying to retell your history and recap her faults. There will be plenty of time for postmortems. You are delivering news. Information. Facts.

If you're stuck, try something along these lines, but in your *own words*, please. She deserves better than someone else's words lifted from a book.

"Honey, things haven't been right between us for some time. I have tried hard to make it the great relationship we both deserve, but it simply isn't working out. I'm deeply unhappy, and I don't want my life—or yours—to continue this way. It's time for us to go our separate ways and to find the happiness we both deserve. I'm so sorry."

Keep practicing. When you think you've got it right, ask yourself how would you feel if you were on the receiving end? Practice until you have your own script and you're confident you can deliver it without anger or blame.

Now it's time to do everyone—your soon-to-be-ex Mate, your kids, your friends and family, your dog, and *yourself*—a huge favor, and rip off the Band-Aid. Deliver the news. Quickly. Decisively. Gracefully.

(If your relationship has a history of volatile fighting—physical harm, threats, or intimidation— think about where you will deliver the news and what you will do afterward. Do you need to take precautions against retaliation? The world is littered with men—and women—who have had teapots thrown at their heads, restraining orders placed against them, been falsely accused of assault, locked out of their homes, and seen their bank accounts and credit cards annihilated before they knew what hit them.)

Your Mate may be stunned, but that reinforces what you always suspected: she and you are out of tune.

Regardless of her response, keep your head high, look her in the eye, and stay calm. She may unleash the Four Horsemen—criticism, contempt, defensiveness, and stonewalling—but you will gain nothing, and lose your dignity, if you go there too.

This is not the national debating championship. You and your ex-Mate have had ample opportunity to debate. That door has now closed. The only open door is The Exit.

If you have shared assets—especially kids—exiting your relationship will be expensive and messy. No one has gone through The Exit and bragged about it being fast, easy, and cheap. Be prepared for it to cost you more money than you ever imagined, and for it to be hurtful, slow, and unfair. Especially the latter.

Better luck next time. You both deserve it.

CONCLUSION

CONCLUSION: WHAT NOW?

No book (or therapist) can "fix" you or your Mate or your relationship. The reality is that over 60 per cent of marital problems are never solved, even in happy, stable long-term relationships.

Although the thought of 10,000 hours of practice to achieve greatness in your relationship may seem unachievable and perhaps even ridiculous, greatness lies in small cumulative changes. The best athletes don't usually win by being a lot better than everybody else. They win by being a split-second faster or a quarter-inch closer to the hole than the next guy. In the same way that making a small change in your golf swing can change the ball's trajectory over a distance, small changes in your behavior, words, and attitude can change the trajectory of your relationship.

"But it's not all my fault. My Mate needs to change too," you justify self-righteously. Clip-clop, did you notice the Third Horseman, defensiveness? Let's rip apart this lame defense/excuse.

Firstly, the only Mates who will *not* change are the Dragons. If you chose a Dragon for your Mate, your choice now is to stay or go.

Secondly, let's consider the other 99 per cent of women who are not Dragons. These women are not malicious; they are simply unappreciated. Like you. How's that working for you? Not so great, right?

Otherwise you wouldn't be reading this book. Here's what I suggest to do about it: try leading by example.

Thumb back through the book and grab something that you like. Put it to work. Imagine what would happen if you sent an appreciative text to your Mate once a day. Or if you said, "Thank you for cooking dinner." Or if you tried the seven-minute rule for a week. And then for another week.

Just like going to the gym, you may not see results overnight and it may even hurt a little, because it is your s-l-o-w *emotional* brain that is learning new habits, not your clever *cognitive* brain. You'll need repetition, sustained effort, and practice to build up your emotional intelligence with women. As Daniel Goleman reminds us, "It is our responsibility to learn to become emotionally intelligent. These are skills. They're not easy. Nature didn't give them to us. We have to learn to use them."[49]

But if you want to have a great relationship with your Mate—and great relationships with the minority group that represents over half the people on the planet—you now have seven simple steps to get you on your way. What are you waiting for?

I never said it would be easy, I only said it would be worth it.

—MAE WEST

ACKNOWLEDGMENTS

I'd like to thank the many insightful writers, thinkers, and doers who have inspired me in one way or another:

Doug Burns
Stephen M. R. Covey
Stephen R. Covey
Scott Dinsmore
Aretha Franklin
Jason Fried
Malcolm Gladwell
Seth Godin
Daniel Goleman
John Gottman
David Heinemeier
   Hansson
James Houston
Benjamin Law
Peter M. Lee
Spencer Massie
Bernard Mayer
Otis Redding
Jim Rohn
Diane Ross
Dan Savage
Julie Schwartz
   Gottman
Nancy Silver
Sharon Strand Ellison

A big thanks to Darren Donnelly, Chris Fong, and John Young for beta testing my manuscript. Special thanks to Eve and Martin Grelis, Marilyn Job, Madeleine Knowles, and Cynthia Roney who had my back when this baby nearly went off the rails. Thank you, Robby Belland, for your guidance.

THANK YOU
FOR READING MY BOOK

I hope *How To Survive Women: A Man's Guide* inspires you to rethink how you relate to women, especially your Mate, past, present, or future. For those who want to learn more, there are free tools and a blog at www.karenknowles.com. Drop a line to kmk@osbornestewart.com and let me know how it's going. I look forward to hearing from you.

SNEAK PREVIEW

HOW TO SURVIVE MEN: A WOMAN'S GUIDE

...ONE OF US IS WRONG AND IT ISN'T ME

CRITICISM = KRYPTONITE

Your Mate has his shaving detritus all over the bathroom sink and his wet towel on the floor. Or he left the milk out of the fridge again. You're fed up, and it's time to let him know. "You left the milk out again. I'm sick and tired of picking up after you. I'm not your mother. What the hell is wrong with you?"

While it may feel better with that outburst off your chest, this dialogue has been set up to end badly. According to research by Dr. John Gottman, the fate of a couple's fight can be predicted in the first three minutes with 96 per cent accuracy because *discussions invariably end on the same note as they begin.*[50] It is *women* who hold the balance of power to successfully resolve spousal spats because they take the lead in bringing up issues more often than their Mates.

Expecting your Mate to change his behavior after criticizing him is like expecting Superman to leap tall buildings after you wave a chunk of kryptonite in his face. Let's take a look at what is going on inside his brain.

A man's brain perceives criticism and contempt in *the same way* it perceives threats or stressors. When you criticize your Mate, he feels under attack as surely as if you were a saber-toothed tiger.

The natural reflex to a stressor is to shut down the thinking brain and to activate the habitual or automatic brain. In prehistoric times, this reflex served men well by causing them to fight predators or flee from saber-toothed tigers (the "fight or flight" reflex), but it backfires when you criticize him.

Brain research shows that when a person is under stress, his ability to problem solve is reduced by up to 30 per cent. In other words, when you criticize ("attack") your Mate about his behavior and his reaction is, um, kinda clueless, it probably is. And you exacerbated his cluelessness with your verbal kryptonite.

Your outburst will likely trigger a counterattack. "You're one to talk! You dump your handbag and coat on the kitchen counter all the time. Clean up your own mess first, why don't you?" And then his unfairness upsets you, so you retaliate with sarcasm or anger, and it kicks off a downward spiral.

Instead, resist the kryptonite and tell your Mate in a nonthreatening and tactful way what's bothering you.

"Honey, I appreciate that you work hard and put in long hours to support us. You're smart and funny and sexy and I adore you, but you left the milk out on the counter overnight and your shaving junk in the sink. Mornings are tough for me, but you're making it even harder for me to get out the door with a smile on my face. Do you have any ideas about how to get past that?"

Your valid complaint about your Mate`s mess reduces the likelihood of triggering his fight or flight reflex and gives you both a better chance to put your clever noggins together to brainstorm a solution. Save your rants for your sympathetic girlfriends.

ABOUT THE AUTHOR

K.M. Knowles was born in England, raised in Australia, and established a career and a family in Canada.

The author earned a business degree from University of Technology, Sydney and had a successful international corporate career in finance and energy before pursuing professional writing and mediation.

As a conflict engagement specialist, the author has advised people and companies from all walks of life on how to get along with one another in the sandbox.

The author's favorite accomplishments are having raised two kids who turned out all right and having been first guest of honor at a New York book launch. The gracious Hugh Jackman was second guest of honor.

NOTES & REFERENCES

INTRODUCTION

1 Divorce statistics: John Gottman and Nan Silver, *The Seven Principles for Making Marriage Work* (London: Orion, 2007).

STEP ONE: CHOOSE WELL

2 Four minutes per day: Sari Harrar and Rita DeMaria, *The 7 Stages of Marriage: Laughter, Intimacy and Passion Today, Tomorrow and Forever* (Pleasantville, NY: Reader's Digest Association, 2007).

3 Healthier, wealthier, live longer, have more sex: Family Facts: Social Science Research on Family, Society and Religion, "The Benefits of Marriage," http://www.familyfacts.org/briefs/1/the-benefits-of-marriage.

4 Mom's sense of self: Kids Fitness & Nutrition | Kids & Sports, FamilyEducation.com, "Tangled Vines: The Mother-Daughter Connection," http://life.familyeducation.com/relationships/mothers/54197.html.

5 Separate successfully and healthily: The official website for Mark Sanborn and Sanborn & Associates, Inc., "Leadership and Your Sense of Self," http://www.marksanborn.com/blog/leadership-and-your-sense-of-self/.

6 Nerdy surfer guy: Lyndon Stambler, "Talent Pool," *Australian Reader's Digest*, March 2008, p. 69.

7 Bathtub clause: Kurt Vonnegut and Dan Wakefield, *Kurt Vonnegut: Letters* (New York: Delacorte Press, 2012).

8 No agreement on monogamy: TS-Si, "Couples Can't Agree if They Agreed on Monogamy," last modified January 18, 2011, http://ts-si.org/relationships/28591-couples-cant-agree-if-they-agreed-on-monogam.

STEP TWO: KEEP A GOOD THING GOING

9 Communication: Gottman & Silver, op. cit

10 Men versus women word count: Rational Skepticism Forum, "Sex Differences: Linguistics • Rational Skepticism Forum," last modified March 7, 2010, http://www.rationalskepticism.org/linguistics/sex-differences-t1905.html.

11 Connect and acknowledge: Gottman & Silver, op. cit.

12 35% see meaningful improvement: Gottman referring to Neil Jacobson, PhD of University of Washington, Gottman & Silver, op. cit.

13 Couples rarely actively listen: Gottman & Silver, op. cit.

14 Percentage of time communicating: based on the research of Adler et al. R. Adler, L. Rosenfeld, and R. Proctor, *Interplay: the process of interpersonal communicating* (8th ed.) (Fort Worth, TX: Harcourt, 2001).

STEP FOUR: FIGHT FAIR

15 Top five fight topics: Elizabeth Bernstein, "Fighting Happily Ever After," *Wall Street Journal*, July 27, 2010.

16 Loss of friendship and emotional connection: Gottman & Silver, op. cit.

17 Dispute resolution theory quote: Jennifer Lynch, *First Component of an Integrated Conflict Management System: Dispute Resolution Models*, April 2003, (Jennifer is past Chief Commissioner of the Canadian Human Rights Commission), http://www.mediate.com/articles/systemsedit4.cfm.

18 Men's biological response to conflict: Amy Arnsten, "The Biology of Being Frazzled," *Science* 280, no. 5370 (1998): 1711, http://www.cogsci.ucsd.edu/~chiba/Science%20--%20Arnsten%20280%20(5370)%201711.htm.

19 Husband as stonewaller: Gottman & Silver, op. cit.

20 80% of time: Gottman & Silver, op. cit.

STEP FIVE: DO THE WORK: MORE SURVIVAL TIPS

21 Fights about housework: Soap and Detergent Association, "The Secret to a Good Relationship...Keep it Clean," http://www.cleaninginstitute.org/clean_living/1999_national_cleaning_survey.aspx.

22 Husband doing his share: Gottman & Silver, op. cit.

23 Cleaning and marital issues: Bob Berkowitz & Susan
Yager-Berkowitz, *He's Just Not Up For It Anymore: Why Men
Stop Having Sex And What You Can Do About It* (New York:
HarperCollins e-books, 2008)
24 Deeper issues: Berkowitz & Yager-Berkowitz, ibid.
25 Woman's C-spots: McNulty, op. cit.
26 Long lists: Jason Fried and David Heinemeier Hansson.
"Long Lists Don't Get Done," *Rework* (New York: Crown
Business, 2010).
27 Western nations: Janeen Baxter and Edith Gray, *For Richer
or Poorer: Women, Men and Marriage,* Paper prepared for the
Australian Institute of Family Studies Conference, Melbourne,
2003, http://www.aifs.gov.au/conferences/aifs8/baxter.pdf.
28 Not affected by class, education or income: Ken Dempsey,
*Men and Women's Power Relationships and the Persisting
Inequitable Division of Housework,* Australian Institute of Family
Studies Conference, Melbourne, 1998,
http://www.aifs.gov.au/conferences/aifs6/dempsey.html.
29 10 year old boys versus girls: Jennifer Baxter, *The housework
and homework of 10 year olds,* Australian Institute of Family
Studies, Australian Government, last modified July 27, 2012,
http://www.aifs.gov.au/conferences/aifs12/baxterslides.pdf.
30 Stanford scientists and housework: Londa Schiebinger and
Shannon K. Gilmartin, *Housework Is an Academic Issue: How to
keep talented women scientists in the lab, where they belong,*
American Association of University Professors,
http://www.aaup.org/article/housework-academic-issue.
31 Dishwasher expert: IMDb, "Bryan Cranston - Biography",
http://www.imdb.com/name/nm0186505/bio.
32 Once or twice a week: Berkowitz & Yager-Berkowitz, op.
cit.
33 Amount of sex: E. Laumann, J.H. Gagnon, R.T. Michael,
and S. Michaels, *The Social Organization of Sexuality: Sexual
Practices in the United States* (Chicago: University of Chicago
Press, 1994).
34 Sex in a long-term relationship: Berkowitz & Yager-
Berkowitz, op. cit.
35 Sexual exhaustion: Berkowitz & Yager-Berkowitz, op. cit.
36 Talking is intimacy: Ted Spiker, "Have the Sex Life You
Dream Of," *Men's Health Magazine: Men's Guide to Fitness,
Health, Weight Loss, Nutrition, Sex, Style and Guy Wisdom,* last
modified 2010,

http://www.menshealth.com/mhlists/16_ways_to_get_better
_sex/How_Often_Do_You_Have_Sex.php.

37 Not tonight: Clare Goldwin, "Why are so many men losing their sex drive? Men are now more likely to refuse sex than women–and doctors blame everything from the recession to toxins," *Mail Online*, last modified April 3, 2013, http://www.dailymail.co.uk/femail/article-2303648/Why-men-losing-sex-drive-Men-likely-refuse-sex-women--doctors-blame-recession-toxins.html.

38 Feeling guilty: Hugo Schwyzer, "The Damaging Expectation Of Higher Male Desire," *Jezebel*, last modified April 1, 2011, http://jezebel.com/5785910/the-damaging-expectation-of-higher-male-desire.

39 Chubble: Gish and Mimp, *Urban Dictionary*, last modified June 4, 2007, http://www.urbandictionary.com/define.php?term=erectile%20problems.

40 Correlation between age and chubble: Berkowitz & Yager-Berkowitz, op. cit.

41 Underlying medical conditions: Goldwin, op. cit.

42 Other person is responsible: Berkowitz & Yager-Berkowitz, op. cit.

STEP SEVEN: TAKE A STAND

43 Overlook small stuff: Gottman & Silver, *Why Marriages Succeed or Fail: And How You Can Make Yours Last* (London: Bloomsbury, 2007).

44 Divorce prediction: Gottman & Silver, op. cit.

45 Husband's disappointment: Jane E. Brody, "To Predict Divorce, Ask 11 Questions," *The New York Times*, August 11, 1992.

46 Angry with each other: Gottman Private Couples' Retreats: The Scientific Basis for Orcas Island Couples' Retreat, "What is dysfunctional when a relationship is ailing?," http://www.gottmancouplesretreats.com/about/relationships-dysfunctional-divorce-predictors.aspx.

47 Four Horsemen: Gottman & Silver, op. cit.

48 Five years later: Harrar & DeMaria, op. cit.

49 Emotional intelligence skills: Daniel Goleman, *Identify the Script Behind Your Emotional Hijacks*, LinkedIn, last modified June 7, 2013, http://www.linkedin.com/today/post/article/201306070844

58-117825785-identify-the-script-behind-your-emotional-hijacks.leman.

HOW TO SURVIVE MEN: A WOMAN'S GUIDE

50 Confrontation: Gottman & Silver, op. cit.

Printed in Great Britain
by Amazon